Louise,

May this book give you
and your Mother the
strength to tie another
knot in your rope and
hang on!

With Love & Prayers,

Mary Baldwin

Praise for
Wildflower Living

"With poignant stories of real-life loss, disappointment, and tragedy, Liz Duckworth leads us through a process that explores doubt, embraces truth, and renews faith. She demonstrates how to record our emotions, questions, and responses as we allow God to turn our tragedies into triumph. *Wildflower Living* is excellent for personal study and superb for small-group discussion."

> —CAROL KENT, international speaker and author of
> *When I Lay My Isaac Down: Unshakable Faith in
> Unthinkable Circumstances*

"*Wildflower Living* is a gem: poetic, poignant, and penetrating the heart."

> —DEE BRESTIN, speaker and coauthor of *Falling in Love
> with Jesus*

"*Wildflower Living* leads readers along a trail of brokenness where beauty blossoms only by the grace of God. Liz Duckworth's gentle way of illustrating the varieties of personal pain that color the landscapes of our lives encourages readers to follow and listen to her heart along the way."

> —NANCY GUTHRIE, author of *Holding On to Hope*

"In *Wildflower Living,* Liz Duckworth leads us from landscape to innerscape, from wildflowers blooming to wild flowerings within, intimately sharing life, faith, and inspiration through language as delightful as the flowers she describes."

—MARY PEACE FINLEY, author of The Santa Fe Trail
Trilogy: *Soaring Eagle, White Grizzly,* and *Meadow Lark*

"Liz is one pictorial writer. Each chapter in *Wildflower Living* is captivating—with stories so engaging I couldn't stop reading. I'm so grateful to her for showing me just the way to walk through pain, whether my own or when helping a friend."

—KAREN DOCKREY, author of more than thirty books,
including *Bold Parents, Positive Teens*

"As one who was diagnosed with breast cancer seven years ago, I read with intense personal interest Liz Duckworth's revealing account of her struggles with loss, infertility, and cancer. *Wildflower Living* shows us how to confront suffering so that we can emerge from the fire of life resilient and full of faith. A lovely book!"

—BRENDA HUNTER, PHD, psychologist and author of
Home by Choice and *Staying Alive: Life-Changing
Strategies for Surviving Cancer*

Wildflower Living

CULTIVATING INNER STRENGTH DURING
TIMES *of* STORM OR DROUGHT

LIZ MORTON DUCKWORTH

FOREWORD BY JANE KIRKPATRICK

WATERBROOK
PRESS

WILDFLOWER LIVING
PUBLISHED BY WATERBROOK PRESS
2375 Telstar Drive, Suite 160
Colorado Springs, Colorado 80920
A division of Random House, Inc.

ISBN 1-57856-836-6

Copyright © 2005 by Lizabeth Morton Duckworth
Wildflower illustrations copyright © 1988 and 1992 Dover Publications, Inc.

Library of Congress Cataloging-in-Publication Data
Duckworth, Liz.
   Wildflower living : cultivating inner strength during times of storm or drought / Liz Morton Duckworth.—1st ed.
      p. cm.
   Includes bibliographical references.
   ISBN 1-57856-836-6
   1. Christian women—religious life. 2. Loss (Psychology)—Religious aspects—Christianity.
I. Title.
BV4527.D828 2005
248.8'.43—dc22   2004016012

Printed in the United States of America
2005—First Edition

10 9 8 7 6 5 4 3 2 1

To Christopher and Jonathan Duckworth—
May your inner strength and faith
give you the courage to survive life's worst storms.

Contents

Foreword

Some years ago, while reading a pediatric article, I noted the top three needs listed by surveyed parents of premature infants: information, connection, and spiritual support. As a novelist, I see those same three qualities inside each good story I read and remember. Liz Duckworth's story is one of those.

The tale that intrigued me most in this unique book of hope and healing is the one Liz tells about her summer in San Francisco. She won a dance scholarship at age twelve, and her parents had the confidence to let her live in that city for three months, all alone. Her willingness then and now to stretch through uncertainties and loneliness captures the heart of this fine book about what it takes to persevere through struggle and triumph in healing.

We need triumphant stories. Here, Liz gives us a collection that is honest, funny, and metaphorical. She draws not only on her family and faith but on the landscapes of her life. In a world that sometimes seems set adrift with no hope for an anchoring shoreline, Liz offers us a high, dry country of wildflowers whose inspiration stays forever in our minds.

But Liz has also done more. Her book offers a launching point for discussion in couples' and women's groups, and for those facing major illness or dealing with significant loss. Her suggested journaling approaches offer a personal way for each of us to explore our trials inside the safety of a community, a community formed of all who sometimes struggle with the whys: Why me, why now, why this? Her candor and simple wisdom bring meaning to our questions even as we still seek the satisfying answers.

Theologian and writer Frederick Buechner once noted that the work of words is "to seek, to treasure, and to tell secrets." Liz accomplishes all of that with simplicity and grace in *Wildflower Living*. It is my honor to introduce it and her to you.

—JANE KIRKPATRICK, clinical social worker and
best-selling, award-winning author, April 2004

Acknowledgments

I have so many people to thank for their contributions to this book.

Jane Ambrose Morton—mother, rancher's daughter, Western poet, and the one who provided the inspiration and impetus for this writing project.

Richard Morton—father, reciter of classic cowboy poetry, a model of love and courage in adversity.

Linda Hasselstrom—wonderful author, poet, and teacher, who provided me with a road map for my first revision and who generously shared a part of her life through a Windbreak House writers' retreat.

My critique group, who polished those early chapters—Lissa Halls Johnson, Marianne Hering, and James Werning.

My creative cluster, who encouraged and supported my efforts—Michelle Zavala and Doris McCraw.

My colleagues at Pulpit Rock Church, who inspired creativity and spiritual growth—Scott Myers, Donnette Martin, and Kris Johnson.

My friends at WaterBrook Press—Don Pape, who first caught the vision; Erin Healy, expert editor; Laura Barker, who holds the details and the big picture as well; and Ginia Hairston, a solid rock of support.

Dr. Brenda Hunter—my mentor in cancer survival, who pointed me toward the right books at the right time.

John—my husband and companion along what has been a sometimes rocky path.

Chris and Jon—my boys, who bring me joy and demonstrate life lived to its fullest.

When I began writing at the age of 30, my dream was to write fiction, but I was diverted from that almost before I started. I became enticed by the notion of writing memoir. For over a decade I was compelled by the idea of turning my own life into narratives.... I think many people need, even require, a narrative version of their life. I seem to be one of them.... Writing memoir...is in some ways a work of wholeness.

—SUE MONK KIDD

High-Desert Blooming

There is a time for everything,
and a season for every activity under heaven:
a time to be born and a time to die,
a time to plant and a time to uproot,…
a time to weep and a time to laugh,
a time to mourn and a time to dance.

—ECCLESIASTES 3:1-2,4

What is the season of your heart today?

Are you enduring cruel winds of winter in your soul?

Is your sky covered with gray clouds of doubt and despair?

Maybe this is your season of drought, when the parched earth of your spirit yearns for some sign of life.

In this, your season before the spring, death has invaded and stolen that which you have held closely and lavished with your love.

When you risk loving deeply—a child, a friend, a parent, a hope, a dream—you open your life to the possibility of suffering a devastating loss. Loss may be the price of love, and the parting may cost more than anyone but you can describe or fully understand.

Now you find yourself rooted in the middle of life's prairie, either caught within a raging storm or gasping in the desert of an endless emotional dry spell. Yet you must find the strength to survive. And not just survive but bloom to love and hope again.

Did you know that God has planted promises for us in wildflowers? I've seen them bloom in beauty despite unforgiving climates or poor soil. He's been painting a picture for me of his hope-filled promises following my own losses. His canvas consists of unpaved prairie land dating back to a time when its sandy ground did not coat high hills but lined the bottom of an ancient sea.

Throughout the year I follow a walkway through this dry land and take great pleasure in the vast array of plants that grace it. To me, the wonder of these wildflowers is that they live at all.

A high-desert prairie in winter is as forsaken as an abandoned homestead. Yet I love its bleak beauty and often marvel at the contrast between dry Colorado and water-rich Illinois, where I once lived. Here, where I walk my path down the months of November, December, January, these sad hills spill ragged yucca, gasping cactus, and sandy soil that seems it never has and never will support colorful blooming life.

Then comes the spring, with tender shoots that grow into

green, purple, white, and yellow affirmations of the hope in my own heart.

I'm reminded that your story, my story, and life itself mirror this prairie and its seasons. We each have known harsh times of illness, despair, or death; times of drought or storm that threaten to destroy joy and beauty forever. But our experiences reveal that even a dusty land gives forth treasures if we look for them. Life can bring out the best in us, even after a season of unfathomable loss and grief.

In these pages I invite you to walk with me along the rolling hills that lie at the base of the Colorado Rockies. Let's look down at our feet and learn from the blossoms that tremble in the gentle breeze. Sometimes we'll gaze at mountains capped with snow, subordinate only to a crystal-blue sky. But mostly we'll be searching for nature's gifts that emerge from this dry earth.

> *All sorrows can be borne if you put them*
> *in a story or tell a story about them.*
> —ISAK DINESEN

What does this water-starved earth in southern Colorado's high desert have to teach us? It offers us inspiration prompted by prairie-flower pictures in living color. We can find out about developing a personal root system that will sustain us in drought and nourish us when the rains fall at last.

This isn't a book in which I will tell you how to endure your losses. I don't have "eight easy ways to get through grief"—or even

one easy way. Because it never is easy. Yet survival secrets are yours
to uncover as you read my stories and those of friends who share our
fellowship of loss.

Let me encourage you to explore your own path of pain and
recovery. As you do, I hope you will begin to tell your story and
learn from it. This book is designed to help you journal about your
experiences and unearth the treasures they contain for you. Would
you consider this a dialogue? After you read my words, respond to
my questions in your journal as you would talk to a friend over coffee or tea. We'll tell our stories to each other and in so doing discover
the nature of wildflower living. As you write from your heart,
prompted by the exercises at each chapter's close, you will find that
the key to nurturing inner strength lies in essential elements you can
embrace in your own way.

These elements—resilience, joy, optimism, faith, comfort,
dreams, companions, hope—are gifts from the One who embeds
his very self in his creation. "Speak to the earth, and it will teach
you" (Job 12:8).

The book of Job details the devastating drought and storm that
nearly destroyed a faithful man's life. And how well this scripture
portrays God's role as giver of life and sweet renewal when the Lord
asked Job: "Does the rain have a father? Who fathers the drops of
dew?" (Job 38:28). Be assured that our needy hearts are promised
refreshment from the Father "who cuts a channel for the torrents of
rain, and a path for the thunderstorm, to water a land where no man
lives, a desert with no one in it, to satisfy a desolate wasteland and

make it sprout with grass" (verses 25-27). Study the earth and see how the "wasteland" around you is embedded with prairie-flower seeds just waiting for spring rains to awaken them for all the world to see.

Let's now begin our journey together, seeking unique beauty that can grow only out of scorched earth.

One

Fireweed

Resilience

Fireweed, a long and lovely spire of purple, is the first plant to move into mountain or prairie land that has been devastated by fire. A sign of life and tenacity, it blooms in mid-July, and so Native Americans named it "summer-half-over."

For me, fireweed has become a personal icon, a symbol of the fire of loss that scorched my first experience of motherhood and marked the point in my life when summer moved inexorably toward the fall.

My early years of marriage and work were bright with promise—truly the summertime of my life. I blossomed along with John, my husband and—somehow—a perfect fit, though exactly opposite me in temperament and personality. He is a good-hearted man with a serious expression, one that hides a dry sense of humor. Pessimist to my optimist, introvert to my extrovert, he complements me and knows better than anyone how to make me laugh. Married right out of college and searching for careers, we didn't even think about having children until we'd been married nearly seven years and were living thirty miles west of Chicago.

During the next seven years, our attempts to conceive were marked by multiple disappointments and three miscarriages. Then, our first child, Katherine, was conceived at last. Pregnancy was wonderful. Finally, after such yearning for a baby, I felt her grow inside me. Week followed week, each filled with joy and wonder and dreams of the future.

Yet just a few weeks before she entered this colder world, my little girl found her way into foreboding dreams: images of a tiny baby with a hole in her heart.

Three weeks before my due date, Katherine was born in the panic of an emergency cesarean section, forever dividing my pregnancy into the time that came before—lovely, happy anticipation—and the time after, a time of pain and loss.

This is our journey together…

&

I am all smiles and relaxed readiness in the delivery room, until the moment the nurse does the normally ordinary task of breaking my water bag. Then, sudden panic—the huge gush of amniotic fluid, the prolapsed cord, and the baby's heart rate plummeting.

I am flipped over on my hands and knees, doctors rush in, someone slaps an oxygen mask onto my face. I hear words like "cesarean…catheter…general anesthesia," but I am in a fog from sudden labor pains, the distress of a doctor's hand pushing against the baby's head inside me, and the nightmare of everything going horribly wrong.

John has to watch all this, standing aside, helpless. He tells me later that as I was rushed to surgery he could see my blood splashing on the hospital floor—the result of a prematurely detaching placenta.

Coming out of the haze of general anesthesia, my first question is for the recovery-room nurse: "What about the baby?"

Her voice barely penetrates my consciousness. "The doctor will tell you more."

I feel sure my baby must have died. "What did I have?"

"A little girl."

When I am finally alert enough to be wheeled into the intensive-care nursery, John is waiting for me, wearing hospital scrubs. I've never before seen his eyes so tender or so filled with pain. He describes Katherine's problems: She weighs only three pounds, she has severe heart and breathing problems and other birth defects, her middle toes are fused, her head is small. But she is alive. As I try to absorb John's words, the neonatologist explains the more technical details of Katherine's suspected trisomy 18 genetic defect.

I get my first glimpse of Katherine—my tiny, battered baby covered with patches, a mouth full of tubes for eating and breathing. She looks so frail. I touch her little leg, which suddenly jerks. Seizures, John explains. My love flows to her in waves I can almost see, and my heart bleeds with pain for her pain.

Aides take me to my room, a long way from the maternity ward. Still groggy and hurting from surgery, I can barely get into the bed.

I fade in; I fade out. I meet the doctor from Loyola University Medical Center, a neonatal intensive-care unit near Chicago, one and a half hours away. With him is Katherine in her Isolette, all hooked up. He clearly and gently explains what we might expect. She has a rare birth defect. She will very likely go to heaven soon. His kindness and sympathy lend me the strength to say good-bye to my new baby for a short while. They are transporting her to Loyola by ambulance.

For the next two days, Sunday and Monday, John shuttles between Loyola and Central DuPage Hospital, where I try to recover so they will release me. Despite a steady stream of visitors and phone calls, I'm empty and lonely for my baby. I wake up in the middle of the night thinking about Katherine, crying and missing her. At three in the morning I call Loyola and talk to her nurse, asking about Katherine, wanting the nurse to give her a hug and kiss for me.

Finally, Monday afternoon I learn my baby has had a bad spell. She almost didn't pull through. I can't wait any longer to go to my Katherine. Though I'm not fully recovered from my cesarean, my nurse pulls strings and gets special permission for me to leave. My parents and John help me break away for a few hours. In the rush I realize I don't even have clean clothes, so I borrow hospital pajamas and slippers.

When I finally see my baby again, my heart breaks at her helplessness. Her naked skin is bright pink, and she wears paper eye shields as she lies under a bilirubin light, a treatment for jaundice. She has monitors on everything and is so still, tiny, and vulnerable. The nurse bundles her up and leaves me alone to hold her for more than an hour.

I sit with Katherine in a wooden rocker, her tubes still connected to her air supply and monitors. As I hold her in my arms for the first time, I tell her about herself and us and God and sing her little songs—in a whisper. I love her immediately and fiercely. How hard it is to leave at last, knowing I might not see her again.

Tuesday I am discharged from DuPage Hospital and stay at Loyola as much as possible, night and day. The doctor says Katherine's condition is terminal, and it will be a matter of time, her time. It might be that her heart will just stop working, or she may not get enough oxygen, even though she is on a ventilator. Or we may decide the time has come to take her off the machine that helps her breathe, so she can breathe on her own or else be set free to go to heaven.

I camp out next to Katherine's spot in the neonatal unit, holding, rocking, watching her. Intensive-care nurses help me bathe her and even change her tiny diaper.

Only parents and grandparents are allowed in intensive care, so the days drift by in a unique isolation, father, mother, and child sharing a strange world alone and apart from familiar friends and places.

❧

From my pocket notebook:

> Friday–Saturday. Katherine was taken off the ventilator at
> 4:30 p.m. She breathed on her own! We held her and loved
> her all night long. Finally, at 8:00 Saturday morning, as I
> held her in my arms, she went from this world into heaven.
> A long night for such a tough little fighter. We love her so!
> We'll never forget her beautiful spirit.

The trees that Saturday morning were sheathed in ice, and all the
world outdoors seemed frozen. My Katherine had lived one week.

❧

Four months later we returned to Loyola for a special memorial
service. I wrote in my journal: "Tonight we lit a candle for Katherine Ann—a bright light that symbolized her life on earth, shining
briefly as a brave flame."

The large chapel was ringed with stained glass windows por-
traying the Beatitudes; the first I read was "Blessed are those who
mourn, for they will be comforted." It was a help to be there and
weep freely, sharing the sadness of other people who had lost children in the past months. The list held more than a hundred
names—some twins and triplets, and one set of quadruplets.

Tears weren't long in coming when the service began. A beautiful couple sang a gospel song they wrote about losing their son, miscarried at fifteen weeks. Their faith shone through the sadness, and their music touched and broke my heart.

John and I went forward together when Katherine's name was called. He held the small candle, marked with her name, to the central flame, and then I placed it with the other candles. In the end, all the candles for all the children looked like a birthday cake. In a way it *was* a birthday cake—a light to remember children who have had a real birth into the presence of God.

John and I both felt better afterward, cleansed by opening up the hurt and remembering. After we lit Katherine's candle, we sat, hand in hand, and I was so thankful our pain pulled us closer together.

I wrote in my journal: "Katherine—your life changed us forever. Don't let us forget or hide from what you did for us. Your light should shine as God's own—to brighten the world we must live in...until we see you again."

&

"Let us not beg for the stilling of our pain, but for the heart to conquer it." These words come from Loyola's booklet by and for people who have experienced the loss of an infant. I would return to the thought often as I sought the strength to conquer my own pain and heal from the fires of loss.

In the weeks and months that followed Katherine's single week of life, I cycled through the classic stages of grief again and again, learning that hurt and healing both are part of the natural order of life. My soul felt as raw as scraped skin, and I experienced all my emotions more intensely than ever. Never before had I felt such tenderness for others' losses, my own broken heart a bottomless cup of compassion.

I went to support groups. I went back to work. I went to Katherine's grave and wept regularly.

Again and again I read the words I had underlined in my tattered Bible on March 11, Katherine's birthday: "He pierced my heart with arrows from his quiver.... So I say, 'My splendor is gone and all that I had hoped from the LORD.' ...My soul is downcast within me. Yet this I call to mind and therefore I have hope: Because of the LORD's great love we are not consumed" (Lamentations 3:13,18,20-22).

Heaven seemed as close as my pillow. Whenever the Illinois springtime clouds parted and "God light" shone down, I could almost see my little girl dancing on shafts of light, spinning between the bright beams. I smiled to think of her in the presence of angels, contemplating the day we would be together again.

You don't heal from the loss of a loved one because time passes;
you heal because of what you do with the time.
—CAROL STAUDACHER, *A Time to Grieve*

Hope eventually returned. I laughed again. I reached out to my husband and became pregnant again—with twins. And so in the blackened ground of lost dreams and empty arms, green seeds of healing took root.

It is truly a wonder that growth in nature can occur after severe devastation. A year and a half after the horrific Hayman Fire burned more than 135,000 acres of Colorado mountain land, I drove my red Jeep to the far side of Pikes Peak to view the damage. The fire had burned so furiously and for so many days that it sent clumps of ashes to fall on us forty miles away. Passing Painted Rocks Campground, where red sandstone towers clustered like bereft mothers weeping, I saw destruction around every curve in the gravel road. On hill after hill, burned trees cast such sharp shadows across the bare ground that I couldn't separate shadow from tree trunk.

Yet life insisted on asserting itself there. Along West Creek Road the valley floor glowed with autumn's reds, yellows, and pale greens. In some places the ground spouted tall grasses, while scattered clumps of green took hold elsewhere. Yellow and purple asters still bloomed. A few living aspen lined the road, performing as they always had, turning their trembling celadon leaves to gold. Remains of summer's resurgence, the red stems of fireweed stood like miniature flagpoles, testifying that in spite of the Hayman burn, life would have the ultimate victory.

I was reminded that time is a healer not only of the earth but of one's pain. And the green presence of hope is the first sign of life in any bleak and barren land.

NURTURING FIREWEED RESILIENCE

What is the secret to nurturing a resilience that creates color in the once-gray ash of disaster and loss? Elements we'll explore later include attitudes such as hope and joy, and necessities like supportive friendships and faith. But for me, in the wake of losing my baby, the simple choice to feel my feelings, to experience them in the fullest measure, helped walk me down the path of healing.

When I get hurt, my first response is to numb the pain—in other words, to push away the feelings that remind me of my loss, to hide them deep inside. Avoiding feelings is a common response to grief, but it's not a healthy response. I discovered that when I chose to embrace my feelings—to cry when I felt like crying, and even to laugh when it might seem inappropriate—then I could authentically experience the real world, as hard as it might be. There's one word that perfectly describes this intense emotional intersection of joy (because a loved one lived) and pain (because a loved one is gone). That word is *bittersweet*.

"Laughter through tears is my favorite emotion," says the sassy hairdresser in the play *Steel Magnolias*. I resonate with her statement because honest grief expresses itself sometimes in tears and sometimes through bittersweet laughter. Those who have lost a loved one can become confused at this contradictory crossroad of laughter and pain, but it's important to understand that the contradiction is okay.

For instance, I laugh a lot and I like to make other people laugh. I was gifted with a lighthearted personality and an optimistic outlook. So when I returned to my world after Katherine died, I was a little bit afraid that I would never be able to laugh again. People seemed to treat me with kid-glove sensitivity, and jokes and silliness lacked a place in those early post-Katherine days. But in time, good friends helped unlock the laughter once more.

Our friends Chris and Julie Grant were among the very few who were able to visit Loyola and meet Katherine. Chris and Julie drove John there the day after her birth; they hoped to be able to visit in spite of the ban on all but immediate family. By establishing rapport with nurses and relying on her credentials as a pediatric nurse, Julie talked her way to Katherine's bedside. She brought a little stuffed bunny for Katherine and comfort for John as he held vigil while I was confined to the hospital.

The bravest thing you can do when you are not brave is to profess courage and act accordingly.
—CORRA MAE WHITE HARRIS

But Chris was left behind in the waiting room. Not one to be left out, he devised a bold though sneaky plan. Visitors to the neonatal intensive-care unit were required to surgically scrub and don paper gowns to keep the environment germ-free. Acting for all the world like a medical professional who belonged there, Chris simply donned a gown, scrubbed up, and joined the next group entering the unit, walking with confidence, finally joining John and Julie to see our Katherine.

Chris and Julie helped John take pictures of my baby to bring to me the next day. Next, they drove him to a one-hour photo place and waited while he dropped off the film. They watched while John came out of the photo place and—in his dazed state—mistakenly opened the door of the car behind them, plopping onto the backseat of a surprised stranger. They laughed when they told me their stories the next day, carrying joy into my gloomy room and helping me smile again.

A few weeks after Katherine's memorial service, about to go back to work, I found myself at a mall coffee shop with Pam, a dear friend who had been the point person for communicating my needs to friends and seeing that everything was taken care of during our crisis. We had coffee and a roll at a table on the margins of a busy mall. She asked for my stories of Katherine, and it helped to give her all the details that filled my head and heart. But when I told her about my trip to a toy store to buy a doll-size dress to bury my tiny baby in, I burst into tears and couldn't stop crying. Pam just took my hand and held it while I cried.

When at last she spoke, I anticipated tender words of comfort. Instead, in her sweet and slight Southern drawl, Pam observed, "I bet these people all think we're a couple of lesbians." I just cracked up—and warmed to feel the healing balm of laughter through tears.

MEMORIAL-DAY THOUGHTS

Three years later, on a clear but chilly Memorial Day, I visited the grave of my daughter to think about how her short life changed my own. The pink granite marker reads, "A Gift from God...Katherine Ann Duckworth." Behind the small, square stone, bright silk flowers stood up bravely to unseasonably cold winds and reminded me of the fragile child who taught me about strength in the midst of pain.

She would have been three years old. I often thought of that when I saw healthy little girls at the park. I missed the person she might have been and the times we might have shared together. But I treasured her gifts.

Katherine gave me the gift of compassion and understanding for others who have experienced similar losses. Before she came I would share the heartbreak of people who grieved, but I felt unable to help. I did not know the "right" things to say or do. Now I could put aside my self-conscious fears and simply act when the opportunity presented itself. I had come to realize that some response is better than no response, and I reached out from instincts born of my own experiences. Katherine taught me to become a people helper.

Katherine helped me see that I am stronger than I thought. Having her and losing her was the most devastating thing I'd ever experienced. I thought the pain would kill me. But that heartache wasn't terminal. In fact, once I discovered I could live through this loss, I learned to take more risks in life. I'm not as afraid as I used to be, because I've seen that God will hold me up, no matter how deeply I fall into despair.

Begin to weave and God will give the thread.
—GERMAN PROVERB

Finally, I recognized that Katherine's legacy was alive in my thriving, nearly two-year-old twin boys, Christopher and Jonathan. "What if?" is a question that has no real answers, but it seems to me that if Katherine had not been born and died, we would not have had our boys. My joy in them was magnified because I did not take them or their health for granted. I saw them as miracles who brought me the delight of life each and every day.

Fourteen years later, I still miss my first child very much, but I thank God for the gifts she left behind.

A year ago my friend Jane reminded me that those gifts are hers as well. Jane, who tends Katherine's grave now that we have moved too far away, wrote to me on my birthday:

> I made the trip to Katherine's grave a little late this year. I always think of her week in connection with Holy Week, because I remember so clearly that her memorial service was the day before Palm Sunday. As I watched the children wave their palm branches that Sunday morning, I thought of Katherine praising Jesus face to face.
>
> I don't know how you think of Katherine, but I think of her as the tiny baby I never saw, and I also try to imagine her as the thirteen-year-old she would be. Usually Marie and I choose soft pinks and blues and lavenders for a bouquet— baby-soft colors—but today I put a bouquet of red silk roses in honor of this landmark teenage birthday. They're very lovely; they have droplets on them that look like water, which somehow makes them look real. They stand out nicely against the new snow that I regret to report fell last night.

It's strange to realize that the children who were playing in the school playground just on the other side of the fence the year you chose that spot for Katherine have all moved on, and a new set of students is learning and growing there. It so makes me wonder what Katherine and all those other loved babies buried in that row are doing. Do we learn and grow in heaven? Are they way ahead of us in holiness—grad students to our kindergarten efforts?

Of course, when I think of Katherine, I mostly think of you, with gratitude for your friendship.

Love, Jane

Through her words and actions, Jane has reminded me that learning to connect with another person's loss is a gift that can strengthen others for a lifetime.

Exploring Your Story

Have you gone through the firestorm of loss? Or endured the emotional drain of a seemingly endless drought in your inner life? You have a story to tell, and in the telling you have an opportunity to follow the path to healing.

Take out your journal if you have one—or choose and personalize one just for this contemplation of wildflower living. It can be tattered or new. It can have a beautiful cover or a plain one. Whatever it looks like, it needs to offer space for you to enter your thoughts, your dreams, your memories, your discoveries.

❀ Think about the worst grass fire that ever consumed the once-green land of your life. Now describe it in your journal. Tell of the events and the way they made you feel. Take time to recall the feelings, even those most painful, and give yourself permission to feel them again.

❀ Is there someone in your life who has the courage to share your feelings? Seek out that person for a healing conversation.

❀ Are you discovering gifts growing out of your losses? Name the ones you have begun to notice. Be ready to uncover them fully as you read on in this book.

❀ Think about the fireweed of hope, the first sign that you could recover from the pain and devastation of your loss. Write about the person or event that first brought color to your scorched soul.

❀ Find a picture that reminds you of resilience, and include it in your journal today. Whenever you look at it, ask God to give you the gift of inner strength on your journey toward healing.

❀ Do you feel you lack the courage to go on? How might you act if you did possess courage? Consider one small, brave step you could take today.

Two

Sunflower

Joy

Sometimes called prairie sunflowers, sometimes called black-eyed Susans, these yellow blossoms with round brown centers are common on the high plains. They bloom in profusion along my walking path and quickly spring back to life every time the city weed cutter mows them down. Resembling miniature sunbursts, their flower faces turn throughout the day to follow the path of the sun. And while they like rich soil, they also grow in wastelands and along roadsides.

These flowers lighten my heart; their bright, cheerful faces remind me of life's victories. I think of my son Christopher, whose battle with bone cancer at the tender age of four taught me about springing back to life with determined joy after near-total devastation.

Now, sunflower joy is not some frothy feeling based on glad circumstances. Instead, I define it as a sense of deep peace and trust in God's goodness. Joy grows best in the soil of present-moment living, a condition that frees me from fear of the future and regrets about the past. Joy is a feeling that, like a sunflower's heavenward focus, constantly points my gaze toward the Son—the giver of light and life.

Reaching out for sunflower joy today, I also recall the power of God's love, a light that cut through the darkest of storms and turned my face to him in hope.

❧

It starts…where?

As Chris—only four, about to turn five years old—enters a monumental battle for his very life, clues pointing to this fearful future are vague.

We hear a few comments from Chris, almost asides, referring to his "hurting arm."

He has two bouts with scarlet fever in three months. What child in these modern times ever gets scarlet fever once, let alone twice? None of my friends' kids has experienced this.

Then one night, as he raises his arm to dance with a teenage baby-sitter, Chris screams in pain. *Did his shoulder go out of joint?* we wonder. The pain subsides, but it doesn't go away.

Two days later an x-ray reveals a broken bone. A blurry, scary-looking area on what should have been a clean line of bone elicits no easy explanation from the clearly worried pediatrician. She points out how Chris's left shoulder is swollen, bulging almost. Then she refers us to experts at Children's Memorial Hospital, an hour's drive away in downtown Chicago. We must endure an anxious weekend wait because our appointment isn't until the following week.

The weekend is gloomy and my heart fills with worry that surrounds me like low-lying fog. Our family attends a friend's birthday party Saturday evening. There, as Chris runs and laughs with other kids in the backyard, hampered a little by his new sling, I watch him through a window and wonder what his future holds. Straining to see in the fading light, I somehow know dark days lie just ahead.

On an unforgettable Tuesday in April, we meet with a specialist in children's oncology. The kindness in his brown eyes and the warmth in his voice cannot soften the shocking news. Chris almost certainly has bone cancer. As the doctor speaks, I try to focus on his words, but a roaring sound fills my ears, as if the sea is rushing in to wash us all away in its relentless power.

My mind tries to make sense of what seems completely senseless. *He's only four. He has always been healthy. It's not fair. We've already lost one child. We can't lose another.* I attempt to hang on and listen as the doctor speaks of the future, the treatments available, the odds of winning this deadly fight. And all the while I only want to hold my child in my arms and somehow have his sickness transferred to my own body, so I might bear the fear, the pain, the danger in his place. But the battle is his to endure; those of us who love him can only try in our helplessness to help.

And so life as we have been living it stops short, and a new pattern begins—for Chris, his twin brother, his dad, me. My lively little boy is suddenly plunged into the nightmare of serious illness. That day we all begin to navigate the ocean of modern-day medicine, with new tests coming each day for the rest of the week. Each test draws us closer to an undeniable diagnosis: osteosarcoma, bone cancer.

⁓

Scared, not understanding the tide that has swept him up, Chris first undergoes a bone scan and a CT scan.

"Don't move," the attendants tell him.

"He's only four," I remind them. Wiggly Chris could only hold still in his sleep; how would he get through these crucial tests?

But this is a children's hospital, familiar with the needs of children. The attendants flip on a TV cartoon show, and Chris slowly relaxes on the hard table, mesmerized into perfect stillness while machines scan his bones for their secrets.

As the week progresses, each test becomes harder for Chris and for us.

I stand next to the gurney as he is sedated for an MRI scan on Thursday of what seems like the longest week in the world. No TV show ever created, not even *Power Rangers,* could hold him still for a long isolation in that thundering tunnel. As he drifts off, I encourage him to be brave. My welling tears betray my own overwhelming powerlessness to stop the runaway train of pain and uncertainty bearing us along.

Following the MRI, we arrive home late and exhausted after picking up an abandoned-feeling Jon, who's been staying at a friend's house. He is angry and crying because the only dinner he had was food he didn't like and wouldn't eat. M&M's ease a little of his hunger, but not much of his fear. Late, but at last, Jon and Chris go to sleep, twins in twin beds sharing a room and a life that is about to change forever.

The next day, Friday, Chris will undergo a final test: a bone biopsy—major surgery that will confirm our worst fears. But this Thursday night, as my tired boy with perennially tousled blond hair sleeps like an innocent infant, I kneel next to the bed, nearly collapsing under the weight of my anxiety. I take his limp hand and hold it in mine as I beg God to spare his life. I let my tears fall fast but silently, and I swallow back my sobbing, not wanting to disturb that heedless sleep.

Friday Chris goes through the first of many surgeries, including having much of his upper left humerus removed. This first time, surgeons extract a piece of his damaged bone and insert a plastic tube into his chest to aid with IVs and blood draws. That tube, called a Groshong catheter, will be part of Chris for more than a year to come, snaking out of his little-boy chest, held in place with dressing that looks and feels like strong adhesive tape, to be pulled off and changed once a week, whether it hurts or not.

∼

My little boy wakes up from his first surgery in great pain and greater confusion. For Chris, the usual hospital procedures are hard on him in ways unknown to grownups who have a greater understanding of the human body and are able to trust their doctors as a fearful, suspicious four-year-old cannot.

❧

During one test, a needle poking his skin brings beads of blood that drip down his wrist. Chris shrieks like a tortured prisoner.

"What? What is it, honey?" His screams are terrifying.

"Blood!"

"What about it? Does it hurt?" My calm voice belies the panic stirred by his.

"No! It's blood! When your blood comes out, you die."

How can I make him believe otherwise when the serious disease eating into his bone might indeed kill him?

Another time a nurse tries to make a blood test less scary by explaining as she tightens a large rubber band onto Chris's upper arm: "Don't worry. It's just going to help your vein pop out."

After that, Chris yells and fights each new blood test with a fear I don't understand until later—when he tells me he hates the rubber band especially. Why? Because the nurse said it would make his *brain* pop out.

❧

When chemotherapy begins, the doctors and nurses try their best to prepare my little guy. He is terribly afraid of having his hair fall out. I don't believe he cares about his appearance at age four, so I am puzzled. Later I discover he expected it to hurt. After all, it hurts to have your hair pulled. Wouldn't it hurt more to have it all come out?

Another time I am sitting next to Chris as he sleeps in his hospital bed. Because a blood count showed white cells dangerously low, a bag of red liquid—not fully blood, but platelets—has been attached to his IV, infusing him with strengthening cells as he sleeps. I watch him awaken slowly. He blinks his eyes, then with them opening wider, he traces the tube feeding his central line up to the red hanging bag. He speaks slowly, softly, as a terrible thought occurs to him. "Mom…I think they're taking my blood out."

After I reassure him that the opposite is true, I am struck by the nightmarish nature of his struggle to beat back cancer. In what kind of awful dream world must a child exist, to wonder if doctors might be taking away his blood as Mom calmly looks on?

SNAPSHOTS OF JOY ON THE EIGHTH FLOOR

These were the struggles of a bright four-year-old boy who found himself in a nightmare lasting more than a year, a quarter of his young life to that point. And yet it was Chris, and the children of the eighth-floor cancer ward, who taught me about surviving fear of the future by living in the joy of the moment. Children seem to know that it's okay to cry when it hurts and to laugh and play when it doesn't.

When I return in memory to those fourteen months devoted to

saving Chris's life, I seem to access photographs burned into memory, still shots that capture the hope of not just survival but life lived to its best and fullest measure.

∾

It is Friday, the end of that first, long week of tests. Our new and very young pastor, Ray, arrives in a rush, joining us in the hospital room where we have just been installed with Chris after his biopsy surgery. Admittedly inexperienced and uncomfortable with hospital visits, Ray is here anyway, having battled his way through the confusion of Chicago's traffic and twisted streets. As he walks into the room, I am sobbing. My tears fill his face with distress. "It's okay," I manage to tell him. "It's good news." John explains that we've just learned from the MRI scan that the cancer has not spread. Ray hugs us both, and joy floods the room.

∾

Tuesdays are always clinic days, regardless of whether the day falls on a child's favorite holiday. In my mind I still see the clinic Halloween party on October 31. The waiting room adjacent to the hospital's eighth-floor oncology unit is filled with young cancer patients waiting to be checked in for a week's stay and chemotherapy regimen. A beautiful little girl, maybe six years old, who normally has only wisps of hair, today is bedecked in a curly blond wig, for she is Glinda, the Good Witch of the North. My son is a Ninja boy, a fighting warrior with a black band tied around his bald head. A magician begins a routine for the crowd of kids, and it is Chris who volunteers to be the assistant. I'm surprised to see this showman side of him; he is usually so shy.

Later that night, the kids in their costumes—those who still feel well enough before chemo's hurtful healing triggers nausea and weakness—follow their nurses from room to room. With tubes connected to IV poles, the children manage to carry plastic pumpkins to each room and collect candy supplied by caring nurses who don't want their charges to miss out on Halloween fun.

I picture Chris—far too skinny, but smiling—feeling well enough to hitch a ride on his IV pole, a practical amusement learned from other eighth-floor parents and children. Moving along the hospital hallways attached to a tangle of tubes, a power cord, and a pole is cumbersome indeed…unless you step up on the pole's sturdy wheelbase, hang on for dear life, and let a parent glide you past the line of doorways leading to the playroom. The trip there is half the fun.

I see a favorite photo of Chris: baldness covered by a green cloth baseball cap personally decorated with marker-drawn symbols, his name spelled out in proud, four-year-old-style letters. In the picture he looks tough—okay, even a little sassy—as he flashes a V-for-victory

sign toward the camera. I cannot see that picture and doubt his fighting spirit or his determination to win the cancer battle.

I witness a solemn ceremony in my living room. A circle of elders
from our church have come to anoint Chris with oil, lay hands on
him, and pray for his recovery. This may be another first for Ray, a
former youth leader, now first-time senior pastor. I know it is the
first time he has performed such an act on a shy but stubborn five-
year-old with no hair. Chris is not thrilled about being the center of
attention, and he has been worried about what the oil will feel like.
Will it drip into his eyes? Before he will let them proceed, he insists
on getting a folded paper towel to hold over his eyes. As I watch the
ancient tradition unfold, I'm trying not to laugh because Chris has
pretty much covered his whole face with the unfolded white square,
and he refuses to respond to questions, as if he is invisible behind his
shield. Suppressed laughter explodes through my nose, and I have
to excuse myself before Chris realizes he is being funny.

My most profound mental snapshot is a vision of sorts, granted by
God when I need it most. Only a month or so after his diagnosis,
Chris has already endured weeks-long hospital stays, surgery, deplet-
ing rounds of chemotherapy. He is losing weight, suffering from
mouth sores that defeat any appetite. Nights are filled with wake-
ups, often due to liquid rushing through his system and carrying his

rescue drug, a chemical that combats the chemo drugs and keeps the cure from killing him. I have been at his side during much of this, and now I am exhausted.

I'm driving home from my bedside shift, having handed off hospital duty to John. We have determined Chris will always have a parent at his elbow, no matter what. My path home takes me through crowded Chicago neighborhoods into an empty stretch lining the south side of O'Hare International Airport. The skyline suddenly opens above me as an immense dark bank of clouds surges up from the western horizon. Yet the sky above me is bright blue, the sun beating down with all its warmth through the window. Solar heat warms my face. And it hits me.

> *Listen to your life. See it for the fathomless mystery that it is.... Because in the last analysis all moments are key moments and life itself is grace.*
> —FREDERICK BUECHNER, *Listen to Your Life*

The moment is suspended as if time has stopped, and I know God wants me to pay close attention. I realize the sun is like God and his love, always present, never leaving. In spite of the storm bearing down, he will be there through the darkness and then will burst forth in glory when clouds and rain have passed. I sense he is telling me, "Don't be afraid. Your job is to keep on driving. Just stay on the road. I'll bring you home safely. The storm will pass, and my light will shine again."

In the months to come, I lift my face often to the Light, as a sunflower follows the sun. I hold tightly to the image of sun above clouds, that beautiful moment of clarity in my car. In my darkest hours I recall that God gave me a gift, a promise that Chris would survive his tough time of illness. I find it possible to hang on without doubting the outcome.

Another promise also warms my heart: "Those who sow in tears will reap with songs of joy. He who goes out weeping, carrying seed to sow, will return with songs of joy, carrying sheaves with him" (Psalm 126:5-6).

﹏

God has faithfully brought us all to this present day. My son is a young man of thirteen, not without his scars, an artificial bone, a disabled arm, and questions of "Why me?" Yet, fulfilling a scriptural promise written on his very birth announcement, Chris and I and all the family can attest that "our mouths were filled with laughter, our tongues with songs of joy.... The LORD has done great things for us, and we are filled with joy" (Psalm 126:2-3).

In time we saw God's hand in healing Chris and caring for his left arm, his "hurting arm." An odd thing had happened to the donor bone that had been inserted to replace the cancerous left humerus early in Chris's treatment. Over a span of nearly two years, it just went away. No one has ever explained how it happened. Was it the destructive effects of chemo drugs? Did it just slowly become absorbed into his body? I can't say. We sometimes called Chris "spaghetti boy" because he proudly showed off his ability to spin that left arm in ways God never intended, a trick especially fascinating to new kids he met in school or at soccer.

Something had to be done, but work circumstances dictated a move to Colorado right after crossing the finish line of Chris's fourteen-month chemotherapy course. We searched for new doctors and were directed to an outstanding orthopedic surgeon, a doctor referred to by a colleague as "the best bone guy west of the Mississippi." So God brought us to our doctor in Denver, who chose Chris to be the first person in the United States to receive a new kind of artificial bone, the Phoenix prosthesis developed in Europe. It would allow Chris to have a bone that could be "grown" from the outside so he wouldn't need surgery every six to nine months until he reaches adult stature. The prosthesis has a telescoping piece encased in plastic that melts slightly when exposed to electromagnetic radiation, releasing a few centimeters of growth each time.

His pioneering surgery gave Chris temporary fame on TV and in newspaper reports. His prosthesis is a conversation piece he's proud to talk about and is a constant reminder that he is one special survivor. Today he still endures occasional corrective surgeries, but he is an otherwise normal teenager with an unusual zest for life. He is like a sunflower that has been trampled by the storm but now has joyfully grown back to face the sun once again.

❧

It is fifth-grade field day, and I'm a proud and happy mom, since my son has won the all-important shoe-kick event. Celebration quickly ends, though, and my heart starts to race in anxiety as I watch him get ready for his next competition.

Oh no, I think. *He's in the sack race.* Chris is part of a relay team and third to go. Off he hops with energy and optimism, until his feet tangle in the burlap bag and he falls, hard. He lies on the grass in a crumpled heap for a minute, and it's all I can do to keep from running across the crowded field to help him up. But after a few endless seconds he stands, wriggles himself back into the bag, and hops—hopelessly behind now—to pass the bag to a teammate.

As the race ends, he is crying tears of disappointment and failure, black-marker "war paint" streaking his face. As I dry the smudges, he sobs, "I blew it for my team."

I tell him that he didn't fail his team but showed great courage in finishing his relay leg so his team could stay in the race. I wonder if he believes me.

Happiness is like a cat. If you try to coax it...it will avoid you. It will never come. But if you pay no attention to it and go about your business, you'll find it rubbing against your legs and jumping into your lap.
—WILLIAM BENNETT, *The Book of Virtues*

The very next day is the final day of fifth grade, marking the end of Chris's grade-school years. We both feel nostalgic this morning as we get ready to go to Frontier Elementary one last time. "You had quite a time in elementary school," I remind him. "You had several big operations, got a new bone twice, and made it through some tough medical stuff."

A few thought-filled minutes later Chris says, "You know, Mom, I just thought of something. My time in school has been a lot like that sack race. I've fallen down sometimes, but I always get back up again."

I hug him as proud-mom tears fill my eyes. Like the prairie sunflowers that spring back after weed mowers work their destruction, Chris keeps getting back up. He grows in harsh, inhospitable ground. He is one tough little survivor destined to win the races in life that count the most.

NURTURING SUNFLOWER JOY

Seeking joy in the moment should not be confused with living in denial. I couldn't pretend to be happy about anything that happened to Chris during his cancer battle. Don't think my personal faith was strong during the seemingly endless months when Chris's cancer dominated our family life. Don't think I wasn't angry at the unfairness of it all, stirred to fury as my mother instinct to save my baby spurred adrenaline-charged action. And don't think it was easy to pray in those manic days while rotating work, hospital stays, and homebound isolation.

I was sad that Chris had to miss kindergarten, his first year of school. Even when he wasn't in the hospital, his white cell count was often too low for him to be out in public. Any simple germ could have stolen him away from us.

I grew weary each day of donning surgical gloves to flush his "central line" with a solution to prevent clots. This became my daily job, because John was afraid of accidentally injecting air into his son's veins, possibly killing him. I believed the nurse who promised it couldn't happen, so I took care of that task every day for more than a year.

I ached for Chris every Sunday afternoon, while TV cartoons played to hold his attention, and he tried his best to be still as his father cleaned the site where the catheter entered his small chest. If mishandled, this sterile procedure could lead to infection, hospitalization, possibly death. So careful, precise John took care of that task.

If only we have the courage to let the thunder, lightning, and storm rage and to walk unfaltering in the path of love and obedience to the duty and demands of the present moment, we are emulating Jesus himself.
—JEAN-PIERRE DE CAUSSADE,
The Sacrament of the Present Moment

I found it nearly impossible to pray. But I had the prayers of others to hold me up, prayers I leaned on when bitter winds blew fear and anxiety into my heart. Knowing friends and strangers were praying brought both peace and joy when I was otherwise empty.

Of all the friends and relatives and countless unknown churches enlisted in the prayer battle with us, I counted most on a contingent of children: the children of friends, kids from the fours and fives

Sunday-school class, even the boys' former preschool classmates. Reports of faithful daily prayers sent up to God at bedtime gave renewed comfort and hope.

I truly believe the prayer of a trusting five-year-old "availeth much" and credit these smallest of prayer warriors with Christopher's ultimate recovery and remission.

It is clearer to me now that joy doesn't feel the same as happiness. It may look like laughter or even the bravery of a young child in an unbelievably difficult circumstance. Sometimes joy just feels like a warm blanket and soft hands tucking you in at night. I knew that Somebody was taking care of us, and that gave me the strength to be Chris's mom during the toughest of times.

You can find yourself nurturing joy by trusting yourself to God's care—staying the course and leaving the rest in God's hands. Peace is achieved by taking the very next step forward, and no more. Peace blossoms as you become aware of gifts graciously given, no matter how small. Thankfulness may produce joy to sustain you through the worst circumstances.

An eighteenth-century Jesuit priest, Jean-Pierre de Caussade, painted this word picture of trust that leads to sunflower joy: "It is like the right side of a beautiful tapestry being worked stitch by stitch on the reverse side. Neither the stitches nor the needle are visible but, one by one, those stitches make a magnificent pattern that only becomes apparent when the work is completed and the right side is exposed to the light of day; although while it is in progress, there is no sign of its beauty and wonder."[1]

Do you believe God wants the best for you and those you love? Rejoice in his tender mercies, and look for moments of joy in the midst of whatever you are facing today.

Exploring Your Story

❀ Enter into your journal a list of ten joy-filled moments from the past months or years. Describe them in detail. Then offer thanks to God for the way he is caring for you even when you aren't aware of it.

❀ Consider the children of the eighth-floor oncology ward, kids like Chris who instinctively know how to live in the moment and find joy in it. They become the models from which we adults can learn. Do you seek to be mindful of today's momentary joys? Or are you dwelling in the future and spending too much time on your anxieties residing there?

❀ Respond in your journal to the following words of eighteenth-century renowned Hebrew scholar Israel Baal Shem Tov: "If we were to walk in the woods and a spring appeared just when we became thirsty, we would call it a miracle. And if on a second walk, we became thirsty at just that point again, and again the spring appeared, we would remark on the coincidence. But if that spring were there always, we would take it for granted and cease to notice it. Yet is that not more miraculous still?"

Three

Spiderwort

Optimism

Spiderwort plants, with their pale green, spindly spider legs, are not pretty…that is, until the sun's midday warmth prompts them to open their deep purple clusters to the world. They seek the light and heat, then add bright beauty to spring's plain surroundings. Tough in the face of adversity, scattered among tall grasses, they make me smile whenever I see them along my path.

Spiderworts are my favorite of all the wildflowers in spite of, and maybe because of, the funny-sounding name. With their gawky stems and skinny petals, they seem a little awkward amid the more graceful flowers. They aren't as plentiful as the sunflowers or the spiky yucca plants that dot these plains. And because they are seldom more than a foot tall, they often are lost among the tall grasses of summer.

But their rare appearances provide surprise pleasure, and they teach me to keep seeking treasure in this dry land. I'm always looking for these shy flowers, sometimes hidden away if the day is too young. If I keep searching, even in the mornings, I'll find a spiderwort ready to open its purple eyes and spill glory where it's rooted on the hillside.

That's why I feel so sad when I go walking the day after the city weed cutter has "tidied up" my favorite path. My special few spiderworts are shredded to near oblivion. Yet as my walks stretch over weeks and months, the hardy, happy-faced spiderworts fight back to bud and bloom again before season's end.

This fight-back characteristic of the spiderwort underdog speaks to me of optimism, of striving for life and beauty in the future, no matter what seeks to destroy that vivid beauty in the present. Spiderwort optimism is a characteristic I deeply needed just five years ago, starting one moonlit October evening. That Friday night ended another hard week of full-time work and family work, mothering my high-impact eight-year-old boys. Burning candles from both ends for too many years had left me fried. Exhausted, I started to undress for bed. When had I last felt full and not empty? Unbuttoning my blouse, I thought how stressful life had become...

I'd been moving at top speed since, hmm...when the twins were born. Those first few years were a crazy race through diaper changes, breast- and bottle-feeding, highchair food frenzies, double-stroller mall walks, potty-training trials, and all the joys and tears of learning to be a mom times two.

Then I returned to work full time, and John came home to free-

lancing and full-immersion fatherhood. Hey, it wasn't my fault the
boys abandoned their afternoon naps at the time of that transition.
No doubt they felt Daddy was too much fun to sleep through. But
he struggled to build a writing career while caring for Chris and Jon
and keeping up with their nonstop days.

This is where we stood when Chris was four and we all engaged
in his cancer battle that launched more than a year of unrelenting
stress. In the middle of that year, the company that employed me
was bought by its rival in Colorado. Uncertainty about the future
added to the grind of hospital routines overlaid by worry and fear.
Would John be able to get enough work as a freelancer? Would I lose
my job and our health insurance in the midst of this crisis?

No. Financial ruin was not to be ours. I was offered a good job
with the new company, and we moved from Illinois to Colorado
mere days after Chris finished his treatment and his central line was
surgically removed. He couldn't even swim in motel pools on our
cross-country drive because the wound was too fresh.

Though God in his goodness provided for us, I was tossed into
a whirlwind of change. Before the move, I made many trips back and
forth between states, and on at least four occasions I was gone for a
week at a time while John held down the fort and Chris continued
cancer treatments. I now had a whole new company to understand,
a new computer system to master, a new boss to answer to, and new
employees to manage. I flew to Colorado Springs and checked out
fourteen houses one day, making an offer on one so John could fly
out two days later and give his approval before it became our home.

After we moved, the pace at work kicked into high gear in a competitive, corporate environment with expectations I could never seem to meet. I wanted to get home to cook dinner each night, my last connection to the Donna Reed life that I oddly but doggedly aspired to. Yet this company seemed to value most those who worked late every night. Editing children's books, I felt I should spend some time with my own children, but it was a struggle to eke out the time needed.

One lunch hour, I hustled out of the building toward my car so that I could join the boys for lunch at the elementary school. Hands in pockets, grabbing my keys, not paying attention, I tripped on a rock at the edge of the parking lot and landed chin first on the asphalt. I heard the grinding crunch of two back molars fracturing from the impact. The building custodian was leaving right after me, and when he saw the blood dripping down my red dress as I turned toward him, he hurried me to the lobby for help. A sweet man, if not sensitive, he later confessed his initial panic: "Man, I saw guys shot in Vietnam who didn't bleed as much as you did." Imagine if I'd been wearing white, not red, that day. He might have fainted.

In spite of my pain and shock, I mostly felt sorry about leaving blood drops on the new building's lovely floors, embarrassed that instead of gaining a reputation as "the nice new children's book editor," I would be known as "that clumsy woman who took a chin dive and bled all over the lobby."

I was rushed to the doctor, a gentle woman who consoled me

and gave me fifteen neat stitches, and wore a huge Band-Aid on my chin for a week.

Dental work on root canals and crowns for my broken molars took months to complete. The bloodstains in the parking lot didn't wash away the whole time I worked there.

This was traumatic, right? Well, I had been through so much stress the previous eighteen months that I barely felt any trauma from the whole fall-on-my-face experience. It was as if I could hit concrete with full-body impact and bounce back unscathed, smiling. Or so I believed.

✺

I finish undressing that Friday night in October, and as I'm taking off my bra, I feel a lump in my left breast.

It's late, and I can't bring myself to tell John about my suspicions. I don't want to worry him yet. So I throw on a robe and go outside to unusually warm autumn darkness, where I sit on the patio in the floodlight of a full moon and plead with God. "Please, please, please," I whisper. "Don't let it be cancer. It can't be cancer. I just can't have cancer."

Doubts are the messengers of the Living One to the honest....
Doubts must precede every deeper assurance;
for uncertainties are what we first see when we look into a region
hitherto unknown, unexplored, unannexed.
—GEORGE MACDONALD

I try to push away my fears, a hard task because a stone-cold feeling in my stomach hints that each and every fear is justified.

*

Monday morning I set up doctors' appointments and try to reassure my husband in a calm voice that hides my inner doubts. "It's probably nothing. Nobody in my family has had breast cancer. Don't worry about me. I'll just get an ultrasound to find out, but I'm sure I'm okay."

The optimist in me is about to take a severe beating.

Each test that week adds another cloud to my darkening skies. Painful needle jabs come up empty as my doctor hopefully probes for fluid. No, it isn't a cyst.

Yes, there is something on the mammogram and then on the ultrasound.

Yes, I need a surgical biopsy.

*

The call comes a few days later. I am at work, and when the doctor breaks the bad news, I somehow manage to ask calm questions and take good notes. "Yes," he tells me, "you have fast-spreading breast cancer, now a two-and-a-half-inch tumor." And all I want to know is, "How soon can you take it out?"

Beginning to crumple at last, I call John, who is working at home, and then I flee my office to join him there. We cry together over this new, unwanted intrusion in our lives. It becomes a long day of prayers and tears and telephone calls. How I hate having to break into the ordinary day of family members and friends with my heavy load of dreadful news: positive diagnosis, radical mastectomy to be scheduled soon, chemotherapy to start just before Christmas.

Now there are plans to make, plans to change, a life to put on hold until this next battle ends one way or another. In the midst of this frantic day, I think of a much-admired friend who has been fighting breast cancer with intense nutrition. Will that be me soon? *Oh no!* a voice in my head screams in silent protest. *I don't want to drink all that carrot juice! And coffee enemas are just not an option.*

I gradually realize that I will consider anything, try anything that might beat back the shadow of death.

> *The beyond is not what is infinitely remote
> but what is nearest at hand.*
> —DIETRICH BONHOEFFER

Chris and Jon come home from their third-grade day, and after dinner, as we sit around the table, I break it to them. They seem to know something serious is up before I even speak. "Guys, I have to tell you some bad news."

Chris's eyes grow huge. "You've got AIDS?"

Apparently third-graders have been learning about AIDS this week.

"No, honey. I've got cancer."

Chris heaves a loud sigh of relief. "Whew. I thought it might be something worse."

Laughter crashes through the fear. Chris had beaten cancer. Why shouldn't I?

And so I felt a special kinship with my cancer-surviving son as I underwent surgery that cut out the cancerous tumor. Later, we compared notes about how it feels to have a plastic tube inserted in your chest and the strange sensation of cooler-than-body-temperature liquids infused straight into a major vein. He empathized with my terrible postchemo nausea and admired my bald head after I shaved off some final straggling hairs. "Don't put your glasses on, though," he cautioned me. "Then you'll look like an old man." Ever the comforter, my Chris.

It seemed so much easier to endure my own cancer treatment, which turned out to be merely a fourth the length of Chris's. When he was sick, I had wanted to suffer the illness for him, take on the cell-killing drugs myself. Well, in a way I was now getting that chance.

During my surgery, recovery, and three months of chemotherapy, I continued to be thankful that God blessed me with an optimistic personality. Maybe I was born with it. Or maybe it was Pollyanna. I met her at an impressionable age, through the Hayley Mills film when it aired on *The Wonderful World of Disney*. She was everything I wanted to be at age nine, with her long blond hair and her chipper British accent. She had a way of looking at life that impressed me deeply. Whenever things went wrong, which they did frequently for this poor put-upon girl, she would play "the glad game." She didn't pretend to be happy about crummy circumstances, but she would look for at least one reason to be glad. After a very unpleasant Sunday, for instance, Pollyanna said, "I'm glad that it's Sunday, because then it will be six whole days before Sunday comes again."

So my inner Pollyanna frequently blooms again and again, just like the stubborn spiderwort, and helps me during difficult times by getting me to see them in a new way. Sometimes I despise this tendency, and I know it can be grating on people who are hardheaded realists, like my husband. In dark times, I've vowed that Pollyanna is dead and admit that I've killed her. Then she springs to life with her silver linings, and I'm back to looking at the donut and ignoring the hole.

> *Bad times have a scientific value....*
> *We learn geology the morning after the earthquake.*
> —RALPH WALDO EMERSON

In the case of my cancer treatment, there really was a silver lining that I'm almost ashamed to admit. It was a little gift from the surgeon, a bit of balm for my vanity, a side effect I gladly embraced. You see, after an emergency C-section and a second one to deliver two good-size twin boys at full term, my tummy wasn't what it used to be. And it never used to be all that flat in the first place. I've always been sturdy in that Polish peasant-body-style of the Ambrose women on Mom's side of the family. Not to mention the German women on Dad's side. As my mom kindly pointed out when I was still in my teens, I was "not a frail girl."

So at age forty-three, I had a supply of belly fat that made it hard to wear slacks my size—or much of anything with a waistline. So my wonderful plastic surgeon—charged with performing reconstructive surgery during an operation that followed my mastectomy—was all smiles when he measured my lovely lard stockpile. Because in the TRAM flap procedure, tummy fat is surgically shifted and takes the place of breast tissue. I didn't ask for diagrams, so I don't know how it looks on the inside, but I did end up with a hip-to-hip scar, a flat stomach, and a nice, round shape closely resembling the breast I used to have.

ROAD TO RECOVERY

I asked the question over and over again: "How could I have cancer?" I thought I was healthy—invincible in fact. But it quickly became clear that I had been so busy taking care of everybody else, I had neglected to take care of myself. Now I would never want to imply that cancer is something I brought upon myself. I will say that one theory indicates stress might have contributed to my diagnosis. After much reading on the topic of cancer recovery, this explanation satisfies me, but of course it may not apply to others.

Dr. Lawrence LeShan observes this connection between cancer and immune systems damaged by emotional droughts and storms:

The first thing I found was that up to 1900, the relationship between cancer and psychological factors had been commonly accepted in medical circles.... All but one of the nineteen [major cancer textbooks] I found said the same thing: "Of course, the emotional life history plays a major role in the progress of the cancer".... What had happened was plain. Dedicated nineteenth-century physicians working with cancer patients had none of the sophisticated instruments and devices we have today.... They had to listen to their patients in order to learn what was going on. And in this listening, they heard about the patient's feelings and history. The factors of great emotional loss and hopelessness occurring before the first signs of the cancer were so repetitive and frequent that they could not be ignored.[1]

Dr. LeShan's book influenced me greatly as I worked my way through chemo and recovery. He asserts that cancer patients face a better chance for remission and complete recovery if they can structure their lives to exercise their God-given gifts and fulfill their deepest dreams.

As I read these words of his, I caught a vision for living differently:

What we have learned about mobilizing the immune system and bringing it to the aid of the medical treatment sounds simple, but it is often difficult to do.... It means looking at yourself and asking, What is my unique and individual best way of living, of relating to others, of being with myself, of expressing my creativity? How, given that I live in a real world, can I move in this direction? How can I treat myself as if I were really worth taking care of?[2]

Well, it was apparently time to lavish some attention on myself. You know that you've been living full tilt when you spend five days in the hospital and beg for a sixth because the peace and quiet are such a lovely change. That was me—delighted to be unhooked from all the tubes and pretty much ignored by the nurses on my final day before heading back to my "full-catastrophe" lifestyle.

But by then I was better prepared to look at my crazy life with new eyes, as Dr. Jon Kabat-Zinn put it so well:

I keep coming back to one line from the movie *Zorba the Greek*. Zorba's young companion turns to him and inquires, "Zorba, have you ever been married?" to which Zorba replies, "Am I not a man? Of course I've been married. Wife, house, kids, everything…the full catastrophe!"

It was not meant to be a lament, nor does it mean that being married or having children is a catastrophe. Zorba's response embodies a supreme appreciation for the richness of life and the inevitability of all its dilemmas, sorrows, tragedies, and ironies. His way is to "dance" in the gale of the full catastrophe, to celebrate life, to laugh with it and at himself, even in the face of personal failure and defeat.[3]

That sounds a whole lot like the wildflower living I aspire to, learning the art of exhibiting inner beauty and blooming in the midst of drought or storm.

Nurturing Spiderwort Optimism

Cancer put the brakes on my full-catastrophe life and turned it around within a few short months. Symbolically (well, literally) my hair all fell out on the first day of January. It seemed fitting to start the new year with a bare head and fresh plans for the future. But first I had to live through the cure.

My trusted oncologists provided an intense but well-proven course of treatment. The medical part of my treatment consisted of standard infusions of Cytoxan (which literally means cell-killer) and Adriamycin.

These two deadly drugs made me so nauseated that I can only compare it to my pregnancies with Katherine, Chris, and Jon when I experienced severe morning sickness that lasted all day for nearly five months. I could detect hidden scents that even dogs couldn't smell. After each infusion I would throw up constantly for a few days, then go back to work and exist on crackers and a few strange foods that only appealed to me in the week after chemo: peanut-butter sandwiches and Taco Bell burritos (please hold the onions).

The chemo drugs kill all fast-growing cells like cancer cells, but they also kill cells that grow hair, ensuring that for one quarter of a year at least, you won't have to worry about shaving your legs or plucking your eyebrows! There's my Pollyanna, ever the spiderwort optimist.

So my hair fell out, and after a few attempts at wearing a pirate look to work (fringy scarf, dangly earrings, swishy skirts, and boots), I gave up on the effort to accessorize this style and opted for a wig. First, Mom took me for some free hair, generously offered by the American Cancer Society. But most of those donated wigs looked lovely for older ladies and all wrong for me. I found one plain, brown short-styled wig, which might have passed for a bathing cap, and tried it out at work. Professional, but so boring and bland.

Following my second chemo treatment, I was back at my desk feeling sick to my stomach and down in the dumps. I could have blamed the nausea, but instead I blamed my bad hair. What was I waiting for? After all, unlike my previous locks, this hair was disposable! I immediately took myself off to Suki's Wig Shop nearby and found the hair of my dreams: shoulder length, nice and thick, a little on the auburn side. Suddenly I felt I could survive the coming months of baldness with at least a little pizazz, though I'm sure the folks at work were a little startled when I returned from lunch with a brand new head of hair.

At night I prayed and hoped that God would give me a new

start, a chance for renewed health and an opportunity to raise my beloved boys. And I'd fall asleep envisioning the cell wars going on inside my body, Cytoxan blasting breast-cancer cells lurking in my bloodstream or lungs, killing them for good and forever.

Sometimes, when I glimpsed myself in the bathroom mirror before showering, I wondered who this alien-woman was, with her bald head and a plastic tube protruding from her chest. While John continued to be caring and supportive during these difficult days, I know he must have wondered where the wife of his youth had gone.

As my chemo sessions concluded, I was ready to exercise some spiderwort optimism. So I planned my own Make-A-Wish trip. After all, when Chris was sick, caring people played Santa and brought him presents, and Make-A-Wish volunteers gave him a telescope and a personal visit to the planetarium (instead of the trip to Mars and the real space suit he had asked for). So now I wanted my own wish granted.

My high-school best friend, Leslie, and I went to Hollywood and spent an entire day on the set of *ER,* thanks to an old friend who was producing the show. I even got to play an extra (a pink-smocked volunteer named "Joanne Chan," according to the attached name tag) in a scene. Sadly, my big moment was left on the cutting-room floor, but the excitement was more than enough reward for me!

Going to Hollywood for a few days was just the break I needed, just the right adventure to remind me that my life wasn't over and that many wonderful events might lie ahead. It was then that good old optimistic Pollyanna grabbed the reins of my personality and assured me it was okay to laugh and live fully once again. On the trip home I promised myself that I would build a new future and try to become the person God designed me to be.

It was time for a real life change. My husband sacrificed his freedom to work at home and took a job that offered a steady salary and the essential health insurance my full-time work had provided. Soon I took a (very) early retirement and followed my own dream by freelancing. My longtime love of theater found expression through a part-time job directing the drama program at Pulpit Rock Church. I also get to spend a lot more time with the boys and have enjoyed summers with them that I missed before. While life can still be a whirlwind, in many ways it is just the life I would have designed for myself had God not pointed me this way.

I'm not glad I had cancer. Yet so many good things came out of it—changes deeper than the physical scars that altered my body forever. The cancer was a wake-up call, and I'm glad I learned lessons about not just surviving but living a life that is abundant. Surviving cancer helped me discover my soul's roots again and learn to nourish them. Like a spiderwort that blooms among the cacti of semi-arid hillsides, I want to optimistically grow, to reach into the ground below and express the colors that brighten my life.

Thanks be to God for once again bringing me through with his faithfulness and his promises. "I am still confident of this: I will see the goodness of the LORD in the land of the living. Wait for the LORD; be strong and take heart and wait for the LORD" (Psalm 27:13-14).

Your perspective and the state of your heart make all the difference in how you react to deprivation in life. One of my favorite books as a child was *Five Little Peppers and How They Grew.* This is the heartwarming (some might say sappy) tale of five impoverished children living with their widowed mother in the early 1900s. Of course, they were spunky, loving youngsters, generous and kind to one another while bearing up under hard times. In one episode, the Pepper children were given a special treat: butter. In those difficult times, butter was an expensive luxury—a treat to be savored—so they used it sparingly and with great delight.

That story deeply impressed me in my nondeprived childhood, when butter was just a standard part of any sandwich. But these days, when I'm cutting back on butter to control calories, I remember that story and like to imagine I'm little Polly Pepper, spreading tiny dabs of butter on my toast and glad to have it. Suddenly I'm not unhappy about limiting butter; I'm focusing on the glorious gift of texture and flavor even a little bit contributes.

It's a silly game, but this little change of perspective works for me on a small scale. Maybe it could also help you to apply optimism and express appreciation for the large-scale joys offered in the course of your daily life.

Exploring Your Story

❀ If a spiderwort optimist like Pollyanna could look at your life today, what good would she point to? Write about the positive things that have been rooted in the difficult times of your life.

❀ Take a walk around your neighborhood and look at the flowers growing there. You might find spiderwort. You might find only dandelions. But how might studying whatever you find lead you to appreciate what you have today?

❀ In your journal, make a list of ten things you love to do. Then list ten things that rob you of energy and joy. Consider how to do more of the first by giving the second less power in your life.

❀ It's your turn to make a wish. Imagine that six months from now your life can be anything you desire. Where and how would you exercise your creativity and your energies? Where would you live? What would you do with your time? Six months from now, what life would you most enjoy?

❀ Now, what changes can you make to shape your life so it more closely resembles your dreams?

Four

Blue-Flax

Faith

Wild blue flax, a multistemmed, frothy-leaved plant with tiny flowers the color of sky, sways in response to any gentle breeze. Yet its fragile-looking flowers betray the toughness of supporting stems, whose fibers were used by Native Americans to weave baskets, fishing nets, and even snowshoes. Did you know that flax seeds also give us linseed oil, used in painting and medicine? So they are beautiful, strong, and useful too.

Flax flowers are stars in their own way, each with five blue petals twinkling in sunlight, a multitude scattered like the night lights embedded in a clear black sky. They are sun lovers, with tight morning buds that blink open as bright daylight awakens them.

This drought-tolerant flower multiplies readily, and once it takes root, it hangs on tenaciously. From its stubborn roots to sturdy stems to bright blossoms, the blue-flax plant is a high-desert survivor. I have loved it in its profusion as it blankets prairie hills like a blue mist and reminds me of the beauty of faith that will not shrink or shrivel in hardship.

Faith is, in the end, a kind of homesickness—for a home we have never visited but have never once stopped longing for.
—PHILIP YANCEY, *Disappointment with God*

Abiding faith is that state of "being sure of what we hope for and certain of what we do not see" (Hebrews 11:1). It's the kind of faith woven into the life of a woman I know, a person whose beautiful smile and calm demeanor could fool you into thinking she has never encountered hardship or significant loss. Anyone who believes that would be completely wrong about my friend Phyllis.

Driving down a busy street, Phyllis is suddenly overwhelmed by despair and she starts to sob uncontrollably. After ten years of marriage and three children, Phyllis finds her life and self-esteem shattered by divorce. Depression and anxiety have fought for control of her life for as many years as she can remember, and now her dreams of a *Leave It to Beaver* life have been smashed.

During the divorce she had heard promises that everything would be okay. She trusted that she would be completely taken care of. Now she's been hit by the devastating realization that everything is *not* okay. She cries out to God through her tears: *I just can't do this!*

Phyllis was totally frightened. Her faith was not strong, and she was drowning in deep confusion. Typical Christian platitudes held no meaning for her. *The peace that passes understanding?* Where was that? *I can do all things through Christ who strengthens me?* At times Phyllis really could not even function. She would sit, unmoving, in a kind of daze.

Looking back, Phyllis remembers how a tiny bit of faith in God's love and goodness prevented her from giving up. She told me,

Have you ever seen that poster where the cat is just hanging on by its claws? The caption says, "Hang in there, baby!" That was me. My kids were young, and for them I would force myself to get up and go on for one more minute or one more hour. And God took care of us. Abundantly. He used the people of my church to meet every practical need, to provide counseling, or even just to sit with me at those times where I sat in a fog of confusion.

Because I was helped in so many practical areas by the church—with food, transportation, even paying my bills—I was asked to volunteer in the church office while I looked for other work. That was a big step forward for me. To be pulled out of myself and my own problems and have to serve others helped me tremendously, even though I was exhausted and felt like I had nothing to give. To be asked a question with respect or to be asked for help as if I were a sane, normal person who really had the resources to respond was a big boost. They were pleased with my work and asked me to stay.

Phyllis has now been on the support staff at her church for more than twenty years. But that's not where her story ends.

Four years after her divorce, Phyllis felt as if she had become a strong, independent person. She says,

> I think that tiny bit of faith was like the mustard seed in the Bible. That's all the faith a person needs. God took that and started growing it into a tree. My trust in the Lord grew and grew—and my personal relationship with him. I was alone with God, having nobody else to depend on. And I talked to him and he talked to me. And he loved me and he took care of me. And I trusted him. My life was full and new, and I really felt blessed.

Vic and Phyllis were introduced by mutual friends and married in 1988. They had both been divorced and were determined that this marriage would be different. Still, both were surprised, even shocked, by the difficulties of starting a second marriage and blending their families together. The first year or two, Phyllis wondered if she had made a terrible mistake. But the couple worked hard on their relationship and talked through problems without giving up. Every anniversary was like a milestone. They would look back over the previous year and see how far they'd come. "After about five years," says Phyllis, "we began asking, 'How could it possibly get better?'"

It is January 28, 1994. Phyllis receives a call that will change her world forever. Vic, a billboard worker, has fallen. Her breath stops momentarily, and then she is able to ask, "Is he all right?"

A choking voice replies, "No, he is on the way to Memorial Hospital."

A co-worker rushes Phyllis to the hospital. Her thoughts race. What kind of injuries does Vic have? How serious are they? Will he be paralyzed?

At the hospital, Phyllis is ushered into a room. The hospital worker is gentle, the message harsh. Vic didn't make it.

"Already?" asks Phyllis. *That's it? Gone? I can't do anything, say anything, even say good-bye?*

There is silence as professional hospital counselors watch her, waiting for reality to hit. And all of a sudden it does. She can't breathe. As she gasps for air, Phyllis hears a counselor say, "Here it comes."

And then the storm of emotions unleashes a violent outburst of agonizing, wrenching sobs.

Inside, she is pleading, "God, I can't, I can't, I can't. Not me."

Church staff members soon come to be with her. They hold her, cry with her, make necessary phone calls. A social-services worker finds the kids at school and brings them to her as Phyllis frantically tries to reach Vic's mother. When at last the two women are brought together, they embrace. They will hold on to each other for strength for many months to come.

❧

Walking through the door on her first return home, Phyllis is struck by the immensity and suddenness of her loss. The first thing she sees when she enters the house are Vic's dirty athletic shoes on the family-room floor—the shoes he would have put on when he got home. She remembers that they were supposed to go to Pizza Hut for supper today. Nintendo games are scattered near the television. The usual debris of life lies everywhere. Mail. Toothpaste and toothbrush. Dirty Kleenex. Dirty laundry. Change on the dresser.

She struggles to grasp what has happened. Vic isn't supposed to be gone.

❧

Later, Phyllis recognized that she was eerily well prepared for the things that had to be done in the wake of losing Vic. With Vic's father's death less than a year earlier, Phyllis had been involved in every intimate detail of his passing, including the funeral preparations and the aftermath. Watching his father die of cancer had prompted Vic to talk about his own time, whenever that should come, and Phyllis knew exactly what he wanted for his funeral and for his family.

She was better prepared, this time, to be alone, she says. "This was not the first time I had been a single parent. I knew how to do it. I had a job. I knew how to parent my kids alone. I knew how to handle repairs and bills. God in his sovereign, incredible wisdom had given me a boss who was well equipped to support me in my suffering."

Phyllis's boss, Kim, had lost his first wife seven years earlier in a freak accident; she had been hit by a falling tree. Kim and his wife of five years, Laurie, were by Phyllis's side at the hospital and for weeks and months afterward, knowing well what kind of support she needed and when. They realized she would be buoyed somewhat by all the funeral preparations and support during the first couple of weeks, but they also knew that the real challenge would come later when she tried to resume normal life. They knew Phyllis would need to talk about Vic. She says, "They gave me important insights about his personal possessions and pictures, encouraging me to handle them, look at them over and over until the pain turned into a sweet nostalgia."

> *The Promised Land always lies*
> *on the other side of a wilderness.*
> —HAVELOCK ELLIS, *The Dance of Life*

In spite of her sense of preparation and the caring support of family and friends, Phyllis was thrown into an emotional crisis for months. "I was afraid again. I wanted to have faith to be a strong

Christian in the face of adversity. I wanted to trust God, but I was afraid of him all over again, and of course I felt guilty about that. Hadn't I learned anything before? Was I a bad Christian?

"It was very difficult to eat. My stomach was as tight as it could possibly be. I couldn't imagine it hurting any more, and then it would tighten even more. Sleep was difficult, because it would open the door for anxiety attacks. I remember lying on the couch at my mother-in-law's house one day, unable to sit up, totally exhausted and literally starving, staring up at the ceiling.

"I just listened to the radio all day. One song to the next, I was given courage to go on for one song at a time. And every once in a while my stomach would relax enough that I could take another sip of milk. I heard everything from God that I needed to hear in the Christian music on the radio."

❧

It is a typical day at work when, out of the blue, Phyllis is overcome by a severe anxiety attack. Her doctor and one of the church counselors are quickly contacted. The doctor prescribes some medication that helps to calm her raging emotions. The counselor helps her understand the spiritual battle she is fighting. They talk, even as Phyllis is crying and shaking, filled with confusion.

The counselor asks, "Where is God right now?"

"Far away," Phyllis answers.

Then the counselor asks, "Where is the enemy?"

A pause. A revelation. "Right here." Phyllis senses her eyes opening to the actual battle she is fighting. She has hit bottom, and she will get better from this point on. The strength of her faith has been tested, and her trust in God for her future will be woven of hardy blue-flax strands that cannot be broken.

❧

Blue-flax flowers look terribly fragile. They grow from tiny black seeds, insignificant looking and protected by only a paper bulb. But their appearance is deceptive. When a summer hailstorm tried to flatten the bed of wild blue flax I've nurtured in my backyard, the slender stalks stood straight once again within a few days. Soon enough, they burst forth to spread and anchor their sturdy root system in the windblown soil, believing they would grow even though the elements declared it impossible.

Don't they make a perfect metaphor for Phyllis? A petite and delicate woman, she evidences a strength of spirit and of faith that endures through life's most furious storms.

The birth of her first grandchild was amazingly comforting to

If it can be verified, we don't need faith....
Faith is for that which lies on the other side of reason.
Faith is what makes life bearable, with all its tragedies
and ambiguities and sudden, startling joy.
—MADELEINE L'ENGLE

Phyllis. She tells me this new life reminded her of the ongoing circle of life. Her granddaughter was named Victoria, after Vic. And another surprise came soon after: new love, and now a new husband, Al. They've been married six years.

What does Phyllis say about this difficult path she has walked, the storms she has survived? "Life is hard. God is good. Life is really, really hard work. God is very, very good.

"Now all I want out of life is to know him. I know now, deep, deep in my heart that I can trust him. I know now what it means to cry out to God and to know, even as I'm crying, that he will answer. I want to talk to him, to learn from him, to walk through life with him. And be ready to be with him forever."

She cites a verse she holds close to her heart. " 'For I know the plans I have for you,' declares the LORD, 'plans to prosper you and not to harm you, plans to give you hope and a future. Then you will call upon me and come and pray to me, and I will listen to you. You will seek me and find me when you seek me with all your heart' " (Jeremiah 29:11-13).

Phyllis truly is an example of wildflower living—covered with gentle beauty on the outside, supported by the threads of a strongly woven faith in God's love and care. She has held on tightly to the things she has hoped for, known with certainty those promises she cannot see.

She ends her story with these reflections: "This is what I would like the summary of my life to be, down the road—the words to the chorus of a song I wrote many years ago:

For she walked with Him and she wept with Him
And she laughed with Him as they sang.
And she grew with Him and she worshiped Him
And He called her one of His own.

"What I've learned about faith is that it doesn't take much—a mustard-seed-size faith is enough. Just a little faith will keep us looking in the right direction, trusting God for just one more minute, one more hour, one more day."

NURTURING BLUE-FLAX FAITH

You'd think a summer downpour would leave some prairie flowers crushed and broken. You'd be right. Fragile blossoms are shredded in the storm's rage. But the blue-flax plant doesn't die when its petals are torn and trampled. It lives to bloom again, to go to seed, and to start new shoots, reproducing in splashes of joyful color. How can the blue flax do this? Because it has the right root system to support those fibrous stems, which bend yet will not break. It has delved deeply into the poorest soil and can survive both pounding rains and extended droughts.

In the same way, our connection to God provides the root system that strengthens us to lift up our heads and hearts. If you send your roots deep, you can live on with blue-flax tenacity. When life's pummeling storm crushes you, smashes you into the ground, and washes away what once gave you purpose, your roots will keep you connected to a saving source of nourishment. Only the roots will allow you to endure harsh happenstances.

> *But now, this is what the LORD says—he who created you,*
> *O Jacob, he who formed you, O Israel:*
> *"Fear not, for I have redeemed you;*
> *I have summoned you by name; you are mine.*
> *When you pass through the waters,*
> *I will be with you; and when you pass through the rivers,*
> *they will not sweep over you. When you walk through the fire,*
> *you will not be burned; the flames will not set you ablaze.*
> *For I am the LORD, your God,*
> *the Holy One of Israel, your Savior."*
> —ISAIAH 43:1-3

So draw deeply from the Living Water. Let him fill you with the resources of his eternal spring. When it feels as though you couldn't possibly go on, just do the next thing. Reach out to touch one life; dare to take just one step. Move ahead with faith in the unseen, until you reach that place where "rejoicing comes in the morning" (Psalm 30:5) and "death hath no more dominion" (Romans 6:9, KJV).

❧

It has been a tough summer for me and my family—the toughest in more than seven years. My dad was hospitalized in June to undergo leukemia treatment, a frightening prospect given that he'd just passed his seventy-fifth birthday. His weight was down, his energy sapped. After four solid weeks of hospitalization and chemotherapy, he was sent home, only to return six days later with a severe infection that laid him up for two more weeks. He was so weakened that he could do little more than lie in bed, unable to carry on a conversation or walk down the hall and talk with other patients as he'd done before. I tried to visit each day, usually including lunch with my mom and time to bolster her spirits.

Panicked at the prospect of losing my dad, I realized how much his love and steady support have meant to me over the years of my life, especially during my trying times. How much of my confidence has come from the special blessing of a father who is always there, dependable, responsible, caring? For many years I had to live far away from my parents, but I always knew they were there for me in any circumstance. Not everyone can have such consistency in family life, and I recognized how truly blessed I am.

Dad's illness prompted me to wonder if I'd subconsciously put so much faith in my earthly father that I'd shortchanged my dependence on my heavenly Father. For when I do one day lose my dad (though today I'm grateful for his improved health and remission from cancer and hope that day is far away), I will be left—as Phyllis was—with the only Father who will be with me always and eternally. To find my strength in anyone or anything else is misguided and shortsighted.

My father's mortality and my own mortality have been much on my mind lately. As my sons grow more independent and I slowly emerge from the day-to-day patterns of mothering young boys, I am more often reminded that all things come to an end. The state of my soul takes on more importance, and my relationship with God seems more crucial than ever. So I'm trying to find ways of growing closer to him now.

The other day I had a long list of tasks to accomplish. And so I played hooky. The weather was unusually perfect: the Colorado sky bursting with blue, Pikes Peak and the Front Range so crystal clear I could practically see individual pine trees on distant slopes. A simple walk would never do justice to such a day. It was the right day to find my way to the top of Pulpit Rock.

I'd driven many times past majestic Pulpit Rock, a stone out-cropping surrounded by gently sloping hills dotted with scrub oak. It's located in a pretty park, an oasis in the midst of Colorado Springs that watches over a road I travel frequently. Almost as frequently, I'd seen the tiny figures of people climbing the rock. I'd heard it wasn't hard to climb once you found your way to the base, but I'd never had time to explore. Until this perfect day presented itself.

I admit I'm getting a little old for rock climbing, a fact I was reminded of as I gasped for breath while hiking the last stretch to Pulpit Rock's vertical towers. But I made it by pulling on bare roots that poked out of the sandy slope and grasping sturdy scrub-oak branches, hoping my sensible hiking shoes had enough tread to keep me steady. Then, as I pulled myself up stones arranged in steep stairsteps, I felt exhilarated to touch the flat top of the highest sandstone there. I was alone in the quiet—except for an unimpressed little lizard and a few perturbed birds.

Well, maybe the exhilaration was really oxygen starvation, but I was elated to be so high above the world, and I settled myself into a shady nook for a time of rejoicing. I lifted my arms and sang (quietly—thanks to my lack of air). It seemed I was actually closer to God, resting so far above the ground, so close to wispy clouds that graced the sky like angels' wings.

I remembered another such time, when I was an editor—overworked and drowning in stress—sent to a California writers' conference where the schedule was intense from morning to night. After three days I finally slipped away for a stolen hour to wander among the tallest trees I'd ever seen, old-growth sequoias packed into a valley green with ferns and spattered with filtered sunlight. Along the walking path was an old concrete foundation, bare, abandoned to moss. First, I sat down to take in the beauty around me, then I lay back and stretched along its cold length, looking up into the wildness of nature and contemplating my recent efforts to escape from life's problems—and God. Trouble had driven me from him, not toward him. And I needed to find him once again, so I stretched out my arms and asked God to fill me with himself and bring peace to my soul again. I left that spot feeling full.

In both of these beautiful places, I felt I was searching for God, reaching out to him in blind faith, because he had been far away during my times of trouble. Yet I know in reality that's not true at all. While nature makes me feel God's presence more acutely, the truth is, he is always with me. I am the one who looks away from him, who closes the door of my heart in misdirected anger over whatever pain I'm feeling. Getting back to God really means I need to change my viewpoint, open closed eyes, and see that he is there for me all the while. If I can just keep that in mind, I'll know his presence as surely in the middle of my messy living room as on top of Pulpit Rock or in the middle of an ancient forest.

"Those who hope in the LORD will renew their strength. They will soar on wings like eagles; they will run and not grow weary, they will walk and not be faint" (Isaiah 40:31).

Exploring Your Story

❀ What forms the root of your life? Is it that exterior blossom: your elegant taste, your high energy, your volunteer spirit, your hard work, your commitment to friends and family? Or is it something deeper: a faith and assurance that cannot be washed away in storm or withered in drought? Do you depend on the trappings of a life well lived, or are you willing to dig beneath your surface thoughts and feelings to draw on the strength given by our unseen Source?

❀ Contrast a time you drew confidently on your faith with a time your faith was challenged, or perhaps seemed nonexistent. Describe the threads of your life's dark times, then describe how they are interwoven with the threads of light connecting you to God.

❀ In this chapter you met Phyllis. She is like many other women who look lovely and calm, with a beautiful smile that belies painful past experiences. Do you ever wish new acquaintances would look beneath the surface and get to know you for your scars? Is there a Phyllis in your life, one with a story to tell—perhaps in exchange for your own? If you've identified such a person, write her a letter in your journal. Then seek her out as a companion on your journey toward wildflower living.

She who reconciles the ill-matched threads of her life,
and weaves them gratefully into a single cloth—
It's she who drives the loudmouths from the hall
and clears it for a different celebration where the one guest is You.
—RAINER MARIA RILKE

❀ Flax fibers can be spun into thread, which is then woven to create a useful, lovely piece of cloth: linen. Weaving the threads of your life's story is part of your regular journaling work. Consider these questions when you next write in your journal: What threads of faith have been woven into your life to create a strong and beautiful cloth? How might its strength and beauty clothe you in future dark days?

❀ An old hymn written by George Matheson and Albert L. Peace more than a hundred years ago once grabbed my heart in the midst of grief and gave words to the faith I yearned to express. Read the first three stanzas of "O Love That Will Not Let Me Go," and write a prayer of response in your journal, perhaps putting the song's plea in your own words.

O Love that will not let me go,
I rest my weary soul in Thee;
I give Thee back the life I owe,
That in Thine ocean depths its flow
May richer, fuller be.

O Light that followest all my way,
I yield my flickering torch to Thee;
My heart restores its borrowed ray,
That in Thy sunshine's blaze its day,
May brighter, fairer be.

O Joy that seekest me through pain,
I cannot close my heart to Thee;
I trace the rainbow through the rain,
And feel the promise is not vain
That morn shall tearless be.[1]

Five

Creeping-Thyme Comfort

Creeping thyme, a beautiful tangle of petite green leaves and tiny purple flowers, has a strong yet gentle presence on the hillsides. It finds the slightest foothold, then sinks roots in deeply, growing in a cluster that leaves no room for intruders. The patch in my backyard spreads farther each year, fending off invasion by weeds and even the most persistent grasses. Along my walking path I see resilient thyme year after year, growing outward, tendrils spreading to cover the bare places.

Cultivated thyme has long been used by cooks because its savory taste infuses all it touches with rich and complex flavor. I wonder if the thyme I see growing wild and untended started domestically, perhaps seeded by a homesteader a hundred years ago, someone wanting an herb to season otherwise plain and predictable meals.

Not only is it savory, but thyme also has a lovely fragrance. The tender scent of creeping thyme travels far in our dry Colorado climate, and its sweet aroma symbolizes for me God's enduring love for his children—the comfort only he can supply when destruction descends without warning.

While we can sometimes see the storm clouds gathering in the distance, other disasters hit when we least expect them. Could it be that you're living in the aftermath of such a storm today? Like a devastating tornado, this loss is so sudden, so inconceivable, it threatens to break you apart. When it's all over, you survey the wreckage and recognize that life will never again be the same, even after rebuilding takes place. In the midst of such a disaster, we seek a comfort that can only come from a place beyond the limits of our understanding. We need the supernatural love of God. And sometimes only he can prepare us to receive that love.

Perhaps this preparation was at work in my friend Chris Bruzzini, a man who seemed to be seeking more of God at the time we lost our daughter. He was so deeply moved by Katherine's memorial service and a letter we wrote about her that he thought about her loss for many years. He would mention Katherine and remember her birthdays, even as his own three children grew.

Chris and Claudia were active parents, busy with their family, wrapped up in the fun of raising children. I remember their first-born baby, Nathan, who arrived while I worked with Chris—a community-theater actor adept at making others laugh—on a play. We hoped Nathan wouldn't arrive during a performance, and he demonstrated great timing by waiting. Nathan was a happy, bubbly baby, and later a great older brother to Emily and Kyle. He and his dad seemed to share a special bond, closer than most fathers and firstborn sons I'd known.

Community theater took a backseat to my twins, but our families stayed in touch over the years, and Chris and Claudia encouraged us while my own Chris battled his cancer. My friend once told me how sorry he and Claudia were to see our family endure so many difficulties. They believed that God never gave people more than they could handle, and Chris expressed admiration for the Duckworth family's ability to stand up faithfully under such pressures. He sheepishly admitted to hoping God knew they could never handle such pressures themselves.

The last time I saw Nathan, the whole family had turned out at a farewell party when we moved from Illinois to Colorado. I marveled at how well this polite and friendly boy seemed to be moving toward adolescence. A snapshot from that gathering shows five family members clustered close together, smiles all around.

A few months later Chris created and performed a one-man show based on material written by my husband, John, which included the account of the birth and death of our Katherine. At one church where Chris performed, a young woman approached Chris after the presentation and identified herself as the nurse on duty who had prayed with us the night our baby died. The shows were well received, Chris told us, though not so much by his own family when he practiced at home. Chris says, "It was hard for Nathan to listen to the story of Katherine. 'It's too sad,' he would say."

❧

It is September of 1999, when I come home from an evening meeting to be met by John, who delivers terrible news. Chris has called, and in a voice so choked with pain he was almost impossible to understand, he said Nathan was dead.

I call Chris back the next day and hear in his voice the unbearable agony of a father whose heart has been ripped in two. As we talk my mind locks onto and recalls our scrapbook photos of this loved and lost son: I see myself bouncing Nathan on my lap—a jolly, chubby baby with a toothless smile; next I see a little boy in a funny skeleton costume at a family Halloween party; finally I remember a well-mannered young man with a quiet smile at our last farewell.

My heart breaks as I try to imagine this close-knit family without their oldest child.

❧

This is my friend's account, told in his own words:

Mid-August, 1999: Nathan and I went to the optometrist for new glasses. The doctor saw some swelling behind his eyes. Recommended we seek follow-up. We did.

August/September: Saw an ophthalmologist and pediatric neurologist, as the working diagnosis was pseudotumor cerebri. This is a benign condition that involves increased intracranial pressure that makes one think there might be a tumor in the brain, but there really isn't. Usually it is associated with headaches. Severe headaches.

Nathan had no headaches. This puzzled the doctors.

September 22, 1999: Nathan had a lumbar puncture (spinal tap). They took the intracranial pressure reading at that time. Nathan's was over four times the normal amount. They told us he might have the worst headache of his life after that. He did. He was in incredible pain. He screamed off and on for the next three days.

We called the neurologist. He said if it continued, to bring him to the ER.

It started to get a little better, and by Sunday, September 26, he was much calmer and the pain appeared to be subsiding. However, he was distant and did not talk much. He told us he did not want to bring on another headache.

Then, on Monday morning, Nathan woke up screaming again. We had a follow-up appointment with the doctor but did not want to wait, so we paged him. He called us back and told us to go to the ER. While I was on the phone, Claudia was trying to get Nathan to go up the basement stairs and out to the car, when he walked right into the wall. I hung up, we got Nathan to the top of the stairs, and he collapsed. He did not appear to be able to see. We somehow got him into the minivan and sped off to Lutheran General ER.

Later that day we learned he had had a "bleed" in his brain and some "strokes." He was still able to talk that first

day, but "obtunded" (the hospital's term, which I later
learned means "lessened").

Tests, tests, tests…

Relatives in and out of the room…

Desperation.

Exasperation.

Pleading.

Quiet despair.

All of these followed.

They did an angiogram of the vessels in his brain, and the
diagnosis was vasculitis (inflammation/infection of the vessels).

Around 10 a.m. on Wednesday, September 29, they
pronounced Nathan brain-dead. It took all day to find
recipients for his organs. The autopsy revealed no vasculitis.

We met with the doctors to ask for an explanation of why
our son died. No one had any answers. One doctor insisted
vasculitis was present. The autopsy doctor insisted it was not.

Pseudotumor cerebri does not generally kill people. It
usually just goes away, but I have found Web sites of people
afflicted with it who are in amazing amounts of pain. I have
not been to those Web sites in years.

Nathan is gone as we knew him. He is with God now.

Within a few short days, a happy family was shattered forever,
a father-son bond was broken in the here and now, and both Chris
and Claudia were living through a parent's worst nightmare. In

those early weeks and months, Chris sometimes wondered how he could go on living.

∽

Some comfort is small comfort; some is as encompassing as a warm embrace. In times of terrible loss, we find comfort where we can. And part of that healing involves looking to find meaning in our pain so that we can become living testimonies of the memory of those we have loved and lost.

How did Chris survive the pain that was so crushing he once thought it might kill him? A supernatural comfort reached out for him.

In the beginning I physically felt God's presence in my life, as if I were being actually supported and held by someone. I feel it now sometimes when I can't deal with things.

Here's a scripture a friend shared with me at the time of Nathan's death: "The LORD is close to the brokenhearted and saves those who are crushed in spirit" (Psalm 34:18).

God is close to me. Spiritual gifts of peace and grace are mine when I want him enough. Although I struggle with my emotions and spirituality sometimes, I have to face the fact that I am powerless over these. I am no match for them. But runaway emotions and doubting spirituality are no match for almighty God. I turn it all over to his loving care. Since I've been doing that, he's taken very good care of me.

The comfort of God didn't shield Chris from the emotional fallout of losing Nathan. "I was angry at everything, especially God, wondering what I had done. I know it's not really about me, but I took it personally." But as time went on, Chris found his broken heart held deep compassion for other people who were living through their own losses. He began reaching out to others with letters, conversations, and books. Though it didn't come easily, Chris made a deliberate effort to become the giving person that he is today. "Although my selfishness can threaten to intrude, I have to look for options that allow me to be of service," he says. "I find that doing for others truly is an enhanced boomerang. Whatever I throw out, comes back. And not only does it come back, but it appears to multiply."

> *Sorrow fully accepted brings its own gifts.*
> *For there is an alchemy in sorrow.*
> *It can be transmuted into wisdom, which,*
> *if it does not bring joy, can yet bring happiness.*
> —PEARL S. BUCK, *To My Daughters, with Love*

As creeping thyme reaches out, spreads its flowers, and leaves its scent, so Chris and Claudia let their loss prompt them to reach out to others and offer comfort.

Recently Chris told me, "The main thing I rely on these days is realizing that God doesn't want me to be the way I was when I first learned my son was dead: I didn't want to go on. I try to ask myself, *What if you died and Nathan acted the way you are acting? Do you think you'd want that?* I had to do something positive, to know that his death didn't mean mine as well."

What is it about our losses that pushes us to ask "why?" Is it that we believe if we fully understand the reason, then the pain will abate? I don't think so. Grief forces us to confront harsh truths about life, truths we shield ourselves from in better times. Suddenly a lace cloth is lifted and the scarred wood of reality can't be hidden any longer. We all want to plan our lives and believe our tomorrows will unfold just as we expect them to. The truth is that any tomorrow can bring a sudden change, a wrenching separation, and scars that last a lifetime. And no answer to "why?" gives us enough comfort in such moments.

For me, I knew early on that I didn't want to probe and pursue the "why?" question when it came to Katherine's birth defect and death. But when a friend's brother died of a sudden heart attack, the two of us embarked upon a study that helped us explore our mutual losses and our desire to understand more about God's part in our suffering. The book we studied together was *Disappointment with God* by Philip Yancey. How little did I know, during those lunches and intense talks together, how much I'd need to go back to those ideas in years to come.

This thought-provoking book helped me better grasp the nature of God and grapple with some very hard questions: Is God unfair? Is God silent? Is God hidden? I wanted to know more about this God to whom I had prayed daily during my first pregnancy, asking for a healthy baby, and who had answered no.

The part of Yancey's book that hit me hardest was the story of a man named Douglas who, while his wife was in the middle of a fierce breast-cancer battle, was hit by a drunk driver and permanently disabled. He thought deeply about God's role in human suffering:

> I learned, first through my wife's illness and then especially through the accident, not to confuse God with life. I'm no stoic.… I feel free to curse the unfairness of life and to vent all my grief and anger. But I believe God feels the same way about that accident—grieved and angry. I don't blame him for what happened. I have learned to see beyond the physical reality in this world to the spiritual reality. We tend to think, "Life is fair because God is fair." But God is not life. And if I confuse God with the physical reality of life—by expecting constant good health, for example—then I set myself up for a crashing disappointment.[1]

So I realigned my expectations about life, and the change strengthened me for battles down the road. I stopped expecting God to give me everything I wanted and simply asked him to give me what I needed—his presence in a very real way, his grace for all my failings, his unconditional love.

Some people mistakenly believe that their losses must somehow result from their own faults and wrongdoing. But I never went down that path, never tried to pinpoint what I had done to deserve my losses. I haven't even tried to identify what these struggles were supposed to be teaching me. But I have attempted to bring good out of evil, because that is a way of honoring my Katherine and her short life and my Christopher and his battle to live.

I was helped with these attempts when somebody shared this image with me: Our fallen world is a place where everyone will eventually encounter the effects of mankind's broken bond with God. Imagine a room filled with poisonous gas, representing our world, where evil has inflicted all manner of dangers: illness, accidents, death. If you walk into a room full of deadly gas, you will suffer the effects of the poison. We all live in this world poisoned by a hate-filled Enemy; we all will suffer. This was not the plan God intended. And only his love can comfort us fully, as it infuses our hearts and souls directly.

We can be open to receive this love. And we can actively seek creeping-thyme comfort, a spreading comfort that builds us up and fills our senses with the essence of a loving God. His caring nature is like a savory spice that infuses a dish with delightful flavor inseparable from the nourishment.

Philip Yancey writes that comfort comes not from understanding the reasons for an unfair event like the death of a child. Rather, it comes from faith, from trusting God in the darkness:

We remain ignorant of many details, not because God enjoys keeping us in the dark, but because we have not the faculties to absorb so much light. At a single glance God knows what the world is about and how history will end. But we time-bound creatures have only the most primitive manner of understanding: we can let time pass. Not until history has run its course will we understand how "all things work together for good." Faith means believing in advance what will only make sense in reverse.[2]

Isn't that the same as trusting that God loves us deeply? All I can do is lean into that love and let him embrace me as a father holds a hurting child. I'll still hurt. But the love that surrounds the hurt is like a soft cushion of comfort that gentles me through the pain and allows me to somehow endure it.

The wild thyme along my path goes on growing, spreading over the earth even during hours of darkness. And in the winter, when the leaves get brown, it appears to die. But the hardy plant is still alive, and I have confidence it will emerge in spring. When I crumble a few leaves, I still catch the distinctive fragrance, just as I'm reminded of the fragrance of God's love even when my life turns cold and I can't see the flowers blooming.

RECEIVING CREEPING-THYME COMFORT

My friend Sandy was just beginning to enjoy the excitement of being a first-time grandma, when her beautiful granddaughter, Laura, died of pneumonia at the age of only three weeks.

Immediately Sandy was caught between wanting comfort for her own pain and trying to comfort her daughter. At times she felt helpless. "A grandchild is as special as your own child. While you hurt for your own loss, you also want to take away the pain for your child, just as you always tried to do when they were little. But there's no way to fix something like this."

How did Sandy receive earthly comfort? "Because God isn't here with skin on, he has given us others, especially those who have suffered loss themselves. My prayer group was very important to me. I was comforted by people who sent cards, came to the funeral, and cried with me. Some people at work made an effort to give me a hug and share their own losses. It helped to talk about it because some people—even friends—wouldn't even mention it, which is really painful.

"I was able to be most open with my husband. He's endlessly patient. He never cries himself but lets me get it out, even when I had a few crying jags, which felt like panic attacks, where I could barely breathe."

Sandy also found comfort in the Scriptures. "It's so unnatural to lose a child, and that results in tough questions. Some people think you shouldn't ask those questions, but God welcomes them. It's a circular process in which we question God and his purposes. We may go around and around questioning and working through the mystery until, finally, we get back to who God really is, who we've always known him to be. He's still the same, though our view of him has been severely tested and perhaps modified."

Sandy found great solace in Psalm 139:16—"All the days or-dained for me were written in your book before one of them came to be." She told me, "I especially like the way that's translated in the NLT *[New Living Translation]*: 'You saw me before I was born. Every day of my life was recorded in your book. Every moment was laid out before a single day had passed.' This assures me that God knew how long Laura's life would be and that he was there every moment.

Truly, it is in the darkness that one finds the light,
so when we are in sorrow, then this light is nearest of all to us.
—MEISTER ECKHART

"When you lose a baby in the hospital, you wonder what went wrong, or whether somebody made a mistake. But this passage re-minds me that God is sovereign, is in control, and knows more than we know.

"All those scriptures in the Psalms and Proverbs about how fleeting life is were also strangely comforting. Though they sound cynical, they remind me that it will not be so long before we're all together again."

The promise of heaven is a concrete comfort. "We know our loved ones are safe, free from pain and anxiety. We know we will see them again, and that makes the separation bearable. I'm glad to have other loved ones there and think that surely they know who Laura is."

Sandy acknowledges one of life's hardest lessons: The longer you live, the more likely it is you will experience loss. Yet in some ways, she believes grief is God's gift to us.

You can't really hate grief, because it makes you join the human race. You will recognize the fragility of life.

As I look back over the past fifteen months, I see that God has comforted us little by little, often in small, indefinable ways. Sometimes it wasn't so obvious that comfort was present. As I listen to others talk about their experiences with grief, I'm reminded that God uses different methods for each of us. Some will find comfort in Scripture, some in nature, others in writing, art, running. God knows what we need, and he prompts us to seek healing.

About seven months after Laura's death, I made a startling discovery: I had stopped singing. I've been a singer since childhood. It's my way of expressing joy, as well as my way of coping with the harsh realities of life—disappointment, anger, sadness, grief. But for seven months I had lost my song and had not even been aware of it.

However, though I could not sing, I found that I had been listening to a lot of recorded music, and my choice was interesting; I had gravitated toward the Baroque period. Baroque music is very orderly and logical. There is no logic in the death of a child; the world no longer makes sense. But our God is a God of order, and listening to Baroque music restored that order to my confused mind and emotions. It made it easier to accept that I will never know why Laura died.

I found comfort in knowing that God could have prevented Laura's death had it been his will. Obviously he had another plan for her life. I can't wish she'd never been born so we'd be spared this experience of pain, because we loved her so much and are richer for having known her, even for such a short time. With comfort comes healing, and with healing, scars. Our scars testify that we've been tested in the fire of grief and lived to tell about it.

Sandy is still in the earliest stages of finding comfort and giving comfort at the same time, as she seeks peace in the midst of life's seemingly pointless turns. Farther down that path is another friend of mine, a woman who drew upon supernatural comfort and then found herself called to comfort others.

Driving down an often-traveled four-lane road, Carolyn Nystrom came upon the smashed wreckage of her daughter's car on a busy stretch near Chicago. That's how she learned her beloved daughter—a young married woman, four months pregnant—was dead. In the months and years that followed, Carolyn exercised her strong faith to survive this loss, mothering her other daughter and two sons while nurturing her widowed son-in-law through his grief. Carolyn is a talented, frequently published writer who wrote *A Tale of Foreverland,* a beautiful story that paints a hope-filled picture of heaven. Her work helped complete a circle of comfort, as her book ended up in the hands of Chris and Claudia and their children, providing a promise of that time when they would be together with Nathan once again.

> *Consider how the lilies grow. They do not labor or spin.*
> *Yet I tell you, not even Solomon in all his splendor*
> *was dressed like one of these.*
> *If that is how God clothes the grass of the field,*
> *which is here today,*
> *and tomorrow is thrown into the fire, how*
> *much more will he clothe you.*
> —LUKE 12:27-28

In the end it is in giving that we receive. It is in comforting that we are comforted. Retreating from the world or shutting down our feelings only shuts us down from life, and we become a kind of "living dead." Those we have lost, however, would be the first to urge us to live fully, embracing others, holding out our hands to share hard-won gifts gained in the course of wildflower living.

Exploring Your Story

We all choose our responses to loss.

We can close up our hearts, shut down our feelings, and try not to love because it hurts so much to lose. We can cover up our hearts, retreating behind a wall of compulsive behaviors—overeating, alcohol abuse, even "vegging out" in front of the television day after day, night after night—that seem to blunt the pain.

Or we can fill the fragments of a broken heart with compassion, letting its warmth overflow us and spill into the lives of those around us.

❀ In your journal, draw a picture of your heart. Is it tightly closed, protected against tender feelings? Do you fear the risk of loving that might lead to losing? Or is your picture of a broken heart, pieces opened up like cups to hold the soothing liquid of compassion? What does your heart look like today? How would you like it to be?

❀ What brings you comfort? For me, it's comforting to remember those I've loved. Try to spend time thinking about people you have lost and what they meant to you. Write about how their presence in your life might be like an enduring fragrance, one that lives on through darkness or the depth of winter.

❀ Many of our memories are rooted in and triggered by certain smells. Think about the scents that comfort you, such as the aroma of a cup of herbal tea, baking bread, popcorn popping, warm cookies, perfume or cologne, specific flowers. Choose one to experience today. Write about the memories brought back by that unique scent, and explain why it provides tangible comfort.

Six

*Tansy-Aster
Dreams*

Tansy aster, a yellow disc surrounded by light violet rays, is among the last wildflowers to bloom in summer and lives well into fall's frosty days. Profuse in many places, the asters' purple color provides the last bright spots splashing my walking path's shoulder before bleak winter returns.

This delicate-looking perennial is anchored by a deep taproot, and its woody, multibranched stem is crowned by what resembles purple daisies. But what is most special about the tansy aster is the way it spreads in disturbed ground around picnic areas, in fields, and throughout open woods.

The aster's spiky glory reminds me that even where the grounds of my life have been trampled, torn, or chilled by coming winter, I can keep pursuing passions and dreams that bring color once again.

I'm also reminded of the inspiring story of my late Great Aunt Frances, who left behind a legacy: a challenge to dare to dream even after heartbreaking loss.

Frances was my grandmother's little sister. When her much-loved husband, Douglas, died from anthrax—he was vaccinating cattle in Texas during the Depression—she was left alone to raise a baby daughter and a four-year-old son. Douglas had been her only true love, and she would never give her heart to another. So Aunt Frances worked as a schoolteacher and reared her children on her own in the small Colorado plains town of Fort Morgan.

> *Go confidently in the direction of your dreams!*
> *Live the life you've imagined.*
> *As you simplify your life, the laws of the universe will be simpler.*
> —HENRY DAVID THOREAU

In her retirement she scrimped and saved to travel to foreign countries with each of her five grandchildren. Memories of these adventures provided a joyful contribution to the memorial service where we celebrated her life. Second-cousin Robert warmly recounted their houseboat stay on the Amazon River, deep in the rain forest, and how much his grandmother's focused attention meant in the midst of his adolescent upheaval.

Though her life was often a lonely struggle, Frances found a way to give back to her family and fulfill her dreams too. She even took the time to bless me with a constant reminder of my own Grandma Ambrose, who died from cancer two years before my twins were born. I'll never forget opening a package with two of the brightest baby blankets ever seen, crocheted from leftover yarn scraps (maybe dating back to the seventies, judging by the vivid fluorescent greens and oranges). Frances's note explained that she had found the yarn, left over from Grandma's projects, and she wanted to make them on behalf of her sister, who would have done so had she lived to see her twin great-grandsons. She told me not to protect these sturdy treasures; she wanted the boys to get them dirty, drag them around, enjoy them fully. And so they did.

My last memory of Great Aunt Frances is during a family visit to Bent's Old Fort, a re-created outpost in southwestern Colorado. As the boy second-cousins played pioneers with popguns, Frances walked along slowly, a stately white-haired woman who never lost her perfect posture. Her son Doug supported her as they strolled arm in arm, and she drifted in the half-dream state of early Alzheimer's. On this picture-perfect day, she was surrounded by children, grandchildren, great-grandchildren, and the legacy of a beloved mother who lived out new dreams when her early dream of a lifelong marriage was destroyed.

The day finally came when dreaming was all Great Aunt Frances could do. Sadly, in her last years, when her mind slipped and her body stubbornly hung on, she dreamed of death, wanting most to leave this world and reunite—after so very many years—with her husband, Doug, in heaven. Now I know they are together as they promised to be forever when they took their wedding vows under the flag on Lookout Mountain on June 7, 1929.

I want to be like my Aunt Frances. No matter what life's circumstances hand out, I hope to continue to give and grow and follow my dreams. Because that truly is living. The other choice requires me to give up and die on the inside, numbing myself to the pain, seeking safety by avoiding the risk-taking required of a life lived fully.

It's hard to be open in this way. Yes, when you get burned, you try to avoid the fire. But never venturing near life's fire means suppressing your deepest feelings and never loving, because love can lead to loss again. It's cold that far from the fire.

A Prairie-Flower Woman with Dreams

Anne Ellis, an unsung Colorado heroine, raised her two children and fulfilled her nearly impossible dream of sending them to college, in spite of her lifelong struggle with poverty.

> *The events in our lives happen in a sequence in time,*
> *but in their significance to ourselves*
> *they find their own order...the continuous thread of revelation.*
> —EUDORA WELTY, *One Writer's Beginnings*

Anne suffered the deaths of two husbands—one in a mine explosion, one from sudden illness—and the loss of her middle child to diphtheria. Though she worked long hours each day to feed and house her children, she still carved out time to run for election and serve as treasurer of Sagauche County, Colorado, in the early 1900s. Her book, *Plain Anne Ellis,* reveals a woman who did not let fear, fatigue, or any of life's losses stand in her way. She writes of her efforts to prepare for her new job and of her struggle to fulfill her duties:

Can you imagine a woman who knew only a sewing machine and an egg-beater, almost in an hour turning to adding machine, typewriter, and calculating machine? A woman to whom a seventy-five-dollar check was big money now handling millions, a woman who had never had a banking account, who did not know how to make out a check properly, now doing daily business and having checking accounts on five different banks?

...It was a frightful fighting time, filled with books and books and more books. The large vault was lined from top to bottom with huge, heavy record books, many of which took both Jean and me to lift. It was appalling. I once invented a sort of tea-wagon affair, and that saved us somewhat. The strain was awful. Many a time have I gone into the vault and, to keep the tears back, bitten my lips until I tasted blood. We worked after hours, nights, Sundays, and holidays, trying to get through the mountains of mail.[1]

Eventually, Anne learned the job of treasurer so well that she ran again and was reelected. That's not to say her life slowed down or became easier. In the rush of her second campaign, she dashed to the printer's office for calling cards to hand out to potential supporters. The printer was in a back room, so Anne called out her request for three hundred cards. The printer called back, asking what wording she wanted on them. Anne disliked the formality of including "Mrs." so she answered, "plain Anne Ellis."

When the cards were delivered, they read:

PLAIN ANNE ELLIS

Candidate for County Treasurer

Republican Ticket

Why did she do it? What drove Anne Ellis to burn the midnight oil and master the maze of politics to do a job for which she was ill prepared? She had a dream and wanted to give her son and daughter the college education she never had. She wrote, "Just a few days ago I wore to the Arizona Biltmore a dress that I made by hand, evenings, ten years ago, when we were sitting at home, Earl getting his lessons, I dreaming and sewing and planning that Earl should go to college. So far as I knew, none of Earl's father's people nor mine had been to college…. I believe this is the power behind most endeavors—wanting for our children what we have wanted and have been denied."[2]

In her book, Anne Ellis calls herself an ordinary woman, but I see her as an extraordinary example of a person who lived a prairie-flower life, striving and struggling and always giving back in spite of her life's pain and deprivation. She easily could have given up, resigned herself to a life as empty as her purse. But she chose to reach beyond her means and in the end gifted her children with hope and skills to enrich their futures. Such is the power of pursuing our dreams.

When I was twelve years old, I auditioned with a host of other young dancers in Denver and won a scholarship to the San Francisco School of Ballet. It was the opportunity of a lifetime, getting to study with the renowned Richard Christensen free of charge, spending my summer after sixth grade at one of the most prestigious ballet schools in the country. But whoever would let a twelve-year-old go off to live in a strange city that was just becoming known for its influx of hippies congregating in its burgeoning Haight-Ashbury district? Actually, my parents would.

That it will never come again is what makes life so sweet.
—EMILY DICKINSON, "That It Will Never Come Again"

As a parent of thirteen-year-old twins now, I'm simply amazed about this part of my personal history. Of course, it was a different world thirty-five years ago, and it seemed perfectly sensible that my folks would drop me off in a downtown apartment, renting a bedroom from taciturn, no-nonsense Mrs. Barrows. I was a responsible child, capable of walking myself to and from the ballet school six days a week, fixing my own breakfasts and lunches, and eating my dinners each night alone at the cafeteria on the corner. Letters home reveal how naturally I took this in, and also what a terrible speller I was for a future editor and writer:

Friday July 21, 1967

Dear Mom and Dad,
Please don't lose any sleep over me not having enough
money. At the moment I have $44.71. Today in ballet Mr.

Christenson picked me out to do eshappe/sotas. I doubt if you can pronounce that because it is spelled wrong. I still don't think he knows my name. He knows I come from Denver. Did you send me the top and pants yet? I do need them. Shall I wash my others at the laundry mat?

Love, Beth

Friday July 28, 1967

Dear Mom, Dad, and Family,
About my laundry Mom: I haven't yet gone to the laundry mat but I plan to soon. Every week I do my wash in the sink so don't worry. Also don't worry about my not having fun. I was board for the last weekends but Valerie and I plan to do something tomorrow. I think we will go to the Planitarium but I'm not sure…

Love, Beth

Tuesday, August 15

Dear Mom, Dad, and family…
Do I have your permission to go to Valeries house and stay overnight? I think I already asked you but I'm not sure. If I get your money tomorrow I am going to go downtown and get my airplane ticket. I had a nice ride Monday when I went down. The Airlines office isn't hard to get to at

all…Not to much has been happening. The weeks have been flying. I ought to be home before I know it.

Love, Beth

Sunday, August 20

Dear Mom, Dad, and Family…

I really had a ball at Valerie's. She has a forest and creek near her house. We went on a picnic and had a lot of fun. We also had a barbeque. Today I decided that I wouldn't get board so I went to the Planetarium and saw the show. The show was the Mystary of Stonehenge. It was really good.

There isn't too much else to say. I'll see you all soon!

Love, Beth

Ho hum—how mundane these letters sound. Just a typical twelve-year-old in San Francisco, making new friends, doing her own laundry, managing money, riding the bus to pick up plane tickets, visiting Golden Gate Park's planetarium on her own. Really not much to say.

Truly this experience was one of the most defining of my whole life. And I'll always be grateful to my parents for entrusting me to the whole adventure, for it gave me an image of myself as a person who could reach out and live her dreams. So many of the challenges I tackled as a teenager, a young married woman, a career woman, and a wife and mother seemed possible because I somehow knew I was up to the task. What a gift to receive as a child on the brink of adolescence! And what a gift to draw upon now in midlife when dreams seem more essential than ever.

NURTURING TANSY-ASTER DREAMS

When hardships come our way, it may seem tempting to abandon our dreams and hold most tightly to that which seems predictable and safe. Is it even appropriate to dream in the midst of crisis and loss? It is.

I've discovered that pursuing new dreams can provide a healing antidote to despair and fears about the future. During Chris's cancer, my greatest dream involved his recovery and a return to a stable family life. When our crisis time eased, my dreams grew bigger and bolder, energized by a new awareness of life's fragility.

Do you have a picture of yourself as a dreamer and a doer? If so, you can use it to fuel your deepest desires and passions. Keep it before you as you take risks and reach out to become all God has designed you to be.

And if you don't yet know yourself in this way, recognize that it's never too late to change. Remember that the tansy aster blooms until the very edge of winter, and you may discover that it takes just one opportunity to grab hold of your elusive dream. Refuse to passively let it go by or bury it as a way of ignoring your pain.

Consider, for example, my friend Jennifer, who always wanted to be in a musical but never took the chance in school and didn't have time in her adult years. Finally, in her forties, she played a part in *Fiddler on the Roof* and loved every second of it. Maybe it seems a small thing devoting extra time for a few months to learn songs and dance steps, but it was a huge thing for Jennifer, who realized a dream at last and discovered it was hers for the taking.

> *Though the fig tree does not bud and*
> *there are no grapes on the vines,*
> *though the olive crop fails and the fields produce no food,*
> *though there are no sheep in the pen and no cattle in the stalls,*
> *yet I will rejoice in the LORD, I will be joyful in God my Savior.*
> *The Sovereign LORD is my strength;*
> *he makes my feet like the feet of a deer,*
> *he enables me to go on the heights.*
> —HABAKKUK 3:17-19

What if you feel you lack the courage, as a result of previous pain, to risk dreaming again? Don't give up the hope that can move you ahead, past the paralysis of the present and into dreams of tomorrow. After my Katherine died, I discovered I had a small bottle of a never-worn perfume called Hope. As days of grief dragged by, I learned to dab on a little drop of Hope as a constant reminder to myself that life would get better and dreams would be possible again. It was a small gesture, but one that encouraged me to move forward.

The famous acting instructor Stella Adler taught an important lesson to her drama students, a lesson in life as much as in performance: "There is one rule to be learned. Life is not you. Life is outside you. If it is outside, you must go toward it…. The essential thing is to know that life is in front of you. Reach toward it…. You have chosen a field where you're going to be hurt to the blood. But to retreat from the pain is death."[3]

Like the tansy aster that blooms in a cold season, your own blossoming can occur even after life's bitter wind blows and autumn arrives. So let your colors show and your petals unfurl, for it is your time to reach forward and risk fulfilling your fondest dreams.

Exploring Your Story

❀ Have you saved any of your childhood letters or diaries? Dig them out if you have. If not, then look at photographs from your past to spark memories. Think of the child you were then, and in your journal write the letters you could have written in real life. What adventures did you wish for as a child?

❀ What dreams have you now fulfilled? List some of your fondest memories of dreams come true.

❀ How have life's tragedies brought your dreams tumbling down? What might be required to rebuild them?

❀ Recapture the child inside, and write about the dreams you hope to make into reality in the years ahead.

❀ Today tansy aster grows profusely in the ground scarred by Colorado's massive Hayman Fire. In your journal, identify the biggest "fire" that has roared through your life, then consider what growth has taken root in that once-barren ground. Write about the equivalent of tenacious tansy asters that brighten your soul and contribute to your inner strength.

> *We are the music-makers,*
> *And we are the dreamers of dreams,*
> *Wandering by lone sea-breakers,*
> *And sitting by desolate streams,*
> *World-losers and world-forsakers,*
> *On whom the pale moon gleams:*
> *Yet we are the movers and shakers*
> *Of the world for ever, it seems.*
> —ARTHUR O'SHAUGHNESSY, "Ode"

Seven

Wild-Rose Companions

I remember the Harison's Yellow rose bushes that bloomed along the dirt drive at Great Aunt Amanta's farmhouse on the eastern Colorado plains. As a child I loved to see those roses in full flower; they failed to wilt even in the harshest summer heat. My mother tells me Grandpa once tried to remove the overly abundant growth, but he discovered it was tougher even than the destructive forces of hoes and herbicides.

Brought by pioneers to brighten the sand-colored land, the Harison's Yellow rose took root and soon grew strong—like its less-pampered cousins in the wild. These hardy rose specimens adapted and spread, not needing careful tending, becoming half-wild as they rooted in a new place.

In my own neighborhood, delicate but beautiful wild roses grow in inhospitable soil, their color and vitality rivaling that of their cultured counterparts. When the last of their pinkish bloom is spent, many prairie roses display round red rose hips, a source of vital nourishment. Most tea drinkers know that rose-hip tea provides a plentiful serving of vitamin C—a gift to feed the body from a plant whose beauty feeds the soul.

The scent of a rose is as much a part of its gift as its beauty. On a warm day, its gentle fragrance fills the air with grace and pleasure, just as the presence of those who love us fills us with joy.

Like wild roses, close friends and family members may help us endure grief and loss. Their stubborn love binds us in relationships strong enough to weather storms of loss and lift our hearts. They are our beautiful companions on the hot and dusty roads we must travel toward healing and strength.

> *Those friends thou hast, and their adoption tried;*
> *Grapple them to thy soul with hoops of steel.*
> —SHAKESPEARE, *Hamlet*

In my life three friends especially have been wild roses in my times of drought and storm. They taught me how to stand by and not back away from those in pain, and how to gratefully receive the help God offers through their loving hands.

Jane Vogel and I worked together when Katherine was born. She had celebrated my pregnancy, though she and her husband were holding back from starting their own family. Jane feared a child of hers might inherit mental impairments, which had appeared on both sides of their family. By nature a question-asker, Jane's candid queries about how I was coping with the death of my daughter helped me talk openly and deeply about my loss.

While some of her approach grew out of her personality, some of it came in reaction to her upbringing. She explains:

> I grew up in a family where some things weren't talked about, including emotions. I have tried consciously to be diffcrent. It is such a relief to have people to be honest with. You can make a lot of mistakes by asking questions, but if people know you are doing it out of concern, they can get past your mistakes.

Katherine's short life had a deep impact on Jane. John and I clearly rejoiced in our daughter and in the way she made us parents, experiencing all the joy and pain of parenthood in a very short time. That example helped encourage Jane to take the risk of having a less-than-normal child. She says, "Seeing you celebrate Katherine's life, even though it didn't match what you dreamed and imagined, helped me see that there is way more depth and strength in parenthood than buying cute OshKosh overalls."

Jane's beautiful, healthy daughter, Marie, was born a year and two months after Katherine spent her brief week on earth. Discovering the part Katherine played in opening the door to parenthood for Jane provided me with more evidence that beauty can grow out of a chasm of pain.

In time Jane found herself deep in grief following her mother's sudden coma and then death from a brain aneurysm. Jane describes her emotionally searing experience this way:

> I remember sleepless nights in the hospital and at my parents'—now my father's—home. I remember agonizing over the decision to remove the life-support systems—a decision we thought we'd made when my parents had made living wills some years before, but which was still wrenchingly hard. I remember the shock of discovering that people removed from life support don't always slip peacefully away within minutes of "pulling the plug": My mother held on for days, still technically comatose, but engaged in a rasping fight for breath that was noisy, ugly, and frightening. I remember thinking daily that without the support of the body of Christ, we would surely have been sucked under and drowned in our grief.

In an article for *Christian Counseling Today,* Jane wrote about those who stood by her during this crisis time:

> We have come to count on the support of friends and fellow church members, and I would certainly never have been able to leave my young family to spend a week in another state without those people who rallied around to provide child care, school carpooling, and the like. But equally important to me were the people who accepted and were willing to

meet my needs that were less obvious, even irrational, but real nonetheless.[1]

One friend took over a work project the two were sharing, finishing it and giving Jane the rare gift of complete freedom from worry about work. Another friend gave her permission to take a break. Jane says,

> Stressed out and sleep-deprived, I confided to her that what I really wanted to do was…go shopping. Even now, over a year later, I realize what a bizarre urge that was to express as my mother lay dying. Perhaps my friend read between the lines to see that I needed to escape, if only for an hour, a reality that was too much for me to handle nonstop. Or perhaps she simply accepted what I said without probing for the reasons. At any rate, she took me out to lunch and to the mall, where we tried on shoes and even giggled at the incongruity of what we were doing. I mark that brief shopping spree—though we didn't buy a thing—as one of the respites that kept me sane.

I so deeply connect with Jane's experience. When my grandmother died, she did so in her home, surrounded by family members. In the course of her last weeks, much of the caretaking fell to my mother, and the burden was growing heavy. Finally, when another relative could sit beside Grandma's bed, Mom suggested that the two of us leave for a while. We ended up at the local library, participating in a craft activity where we learned to make cornhusk dolls. I've kept my doll as a reminder of that hard time, made a bit easier as we busied our hands and spoke of something other than imminent death.

> *It is not, as somebody once wrote, the smell*
> *of corn bread that calls us back from death;*
> *it is the lights and signs of love and friendship.*
> —JOHN CHEEVER

Jane describes another way relationships brought beauty into her bleak experience:

My friends focused on me and my needs. They were concerned for me and grieved for me. But…one thing these friends could not do was grieve with me. While my mother was in the hospital and I was staying at my parents' house, Ruth, a neighbor, delivered a meal. When I greeted her at the door, her eyes welled with tears and she burst out, "I'm going to miss Kay so much!" It said more clearly than anything else could have, "You are not alone." No longer was I merely a recipient of other people's sympathy and care; I was a partner with Ruth in the work of losing someone we loved. She demonstrated that the woman dying in the hospital was someone more than "my mom" to be missed by our family. She was Kay, a friend and neighbor, a woman whose life was of value to people I might not even know.

My family moved to Colorado not long after Jane's mother died, and it was then she offered to be the caretaker of Katherine's small grave. Why would she want to fulfill a task that another friend might find too sad a reminder of hard times? She realizes the value of entering into another's life, the good as well as the bad. And Jane understands that our grieving is different, parallel sharing at best. Yet her regular visits to a grave in Wheaton, Illinois, connect her to her mother, buried far away in Grand Rapids. She says, "I know the grief of losing a baby is different from that of losing my mom. But I realized I could share this feeling of the importance of the physical grave, of having a concrete point of contact, which makes me feel we're in this together, this fellowship of loss."

My friend Pam Campbell is another person who joined my journey of sorrow and helped guide me on a rocky path. She was among the first to rush to my hospital bedside and give me the comfort of her presence. She became the point person for information sharing, coordinating meals and housecleaning, helping in her steady way in the early days and through the years to follow.

How was it she was so able to assist when the need arose? She's not sure herself: "I felt totally inadequate and devastated when I got the news about Katherine. I knew I needed to be there at the hospital but had no clue about what to say and how to help. I sort of went for being in the moment, by listening. I remember that as we talked about the baby, I was conscious that she was your daughter, who was real, with a name, a person that you needed to talk about."

Pam may have been feeling her way at that point in our friendship, but her instincts were right on target. I needed somebody who could hear me and respond to the new and unexpected needs flooding my life. John and close family members were overwhelmed with their own feelings, but Pam provided a strong shoulder to lean on. If only I could have been there for her in the same way when her own time of personal crisis came, not two years later. But I can barely remember her diagnosis of and battle with uterine cancer at the relatively young age of thirty-seven.

Recently I asked about that. Why wasn't I there for her? She reminded me that I had infant twins then, and my world consisted of bottles, diapers, and all-too-short sleep cycles. Then we talked at length about her own journey through the storm and drought, and how it reconfigured her future and the fulfillment of her dreams. But that's a story you'll find in the next chapter.

An author and clinical therapist, Pam knows well that wild-rose relationships work both ways: "We all have parts of ourselves looking for healing. I want to be there for other people, saying things that are helpful. And I want to have someone there for me. We heal ourselves in the way we interact with other people. I approach therapy that way; it's not what I do or say, but who I am. When others have felt massive disappointment, we try to feel with them, watching to see how they deal with it. And we learn from them how to heal ourselves that way."

❧

I like to call my friend Karen Dockrey "The Information Queen" because she is a relentless researcher, and as a widely published author, she constantly asks and answers the hard questions. Her daughter Emily was diagnosed with leukemia at the age of eight, undergoing much pain and suffering before winning her war against this terrible disease. Karen's daughter Sarah battled illness and hearing loss from young childhood and later struggled through the agonies of treatment and surgeries to improve her hearing with cochlear implants.

Karen has suffered life's losses with honesty and reality, unwilling to mask pain with pretense. I so appreciated her loving response when Katherine was born. She sent cards and a handmade cross-stitch featuring Katherine's name and a bunny. How well she knew not to bury the loss, but to celebrate the child we'd had for such a short time.

When she learned my Chris had cancer, she immediately provided me with her list of cancer resources, gathered intently in an effort to deal with her own daughter's illness. It was her method of helping, extending what had worked for her, providing for me what she could out of love and concern.

Karen also talked freely with me as I tried to deal with the "why?" question. In time her own perspective granted me a great deal of peace as we discussed the hurts and losses that fill our world. She reminded me that when the Evil One throws difficulties our way, it is God who is there to comfort and aid us. Karen describes it as a snowball fight, with God helping you while troubles attack from the opposite side. You're hunkered down in your snow fort—crises flying at you like so many snowballs—and you're in the thick of the battle with God at your side. He's not the one throwing the snowballs.

Karen has wrestled with and written about loss in her book *When a Hug Won't Fix the Hurt*. Her wisdom and open-eyed frankness fill its pages—thanks to a heart that wants to help and a spirit that seeks the truth. I'm amazed at how Karen and other friends who have helped me have gone on in varied ways to help others—even numbers of people they'll never meet or know. Thus, a prairie-flower response to adversity brings a bloom of color to the world that desperately needs it.

WELCOMING WILD-ROSE COMPANIONS

In the darkest moments of my hardest times, light came in the form of people who demonstrated God's love and were not too busy or afraid to help when I was most needy. These people brought flowers and meals, cleaned my dirty house, and entered into my out-of-kilter, newly chaotic, often aching world. They called each other and cried together on the phone. They entered my confusing world of commingled pain and joy.

Receiving this love and companionship doesn't always come easily, however. When we are in pain, we may feel like shriveling and fading away rather than allowing ourselves to be embraced. We don't want to be any trouble. Our pride may prevent us from admitting our need. We may not have the strength to interface with well-meaning but unhelpful friends. Like Grandpa's yellow roses, our relationships may sometimes seem overwhelming and unwieldy.

Author C. S. Lewis eloquently described his feelings of grief and their effect on relationships in the aftermath of his wife's death:

> No one ever told me that grief felt so like fear…the same
> fluttering in the stomach, the same restlessness, the yawn-
> ing…. At other times it feels like being mildly drunk or
> concussed. There is a sort of invisible blanket between the
> world and me. I find it hard to take in what anyone says.
> Or, perhaps, hard to want to take it in…. Yet I want the
> others to be about me. I dread the moments when the
> house is empty.[2]

My book editor, Erin, recently described a story she read about a woman who was terminally ill with ALS (Lou Gehrig's disease). The disease was in the advanced stages, and though friends tried to visit, she refused to see them because she was embarrassed by her condition. She relied entirely on her daughter for care. A counselor stated what seems obvious to those outside the situation, "She needs to be prodded a little to see people whose company she'll probably end up enjoying."

What an illustration of how easy it is to withdraw, and yet how important it is to grant others entrance into your pain so they can share it, lift it. The Bible itself reminds us to "carry each other's burdens, and in this way you will fulfill the law of Christ" (Galatians 6:2).

We may not be ready to share our heaviest burdens right away. For Karen, a patient friend was ready to listen when the right time came: "It was four years before I could speak about one of the deepest agonies in my life. But when I was ready, I went back to that friend who had said, 'Tell me about it,' and then patiently waited. She clearly communicated that even if I never spoke about it, she would walk with me through it. It was my need she cared about, and because she freed me to talk or keep silent, I knew I could go to her when I needed to talk."

Jane admits, "I know that some people have a hard time accepting help. I don't happen to be one of those people! I'm probably the only person I know who sends out mass e-mails that begin, 'Dear friends who said you'd be happy to help out if I ever need it—I need it!'

"On the other hand, I've had friends tell me, 'You don't need to…[bring that meal, drive my kid to that appointment, whatever it happens to be].' And I say, 'Yes, I do. Maybe *you* don't need me to do it, but *I* do.' Because when I can't fix the big problem—the child-support disputes or the illness or the loss of a job—I need to do 'something,' even if it's only bringing by a pot of spaghetti sauce. I don't know if the spaghetti sauce—or at least the concern it represents—helps my friend; I do know that she helps me by allowing me to do what I can. And that's how it is that, either way—helping or being helped—I end up being the one who is receiving."

It is not so much our friends' help that helps us
as the confident knowledge that they will help us.
—EPICURUS

To nurture these authentic relationships—the kind where you can drop all pretense and give each other your honest care—you have to be prepared to be vulnerable, exposed. I remember my first thought when my friend Barb offered to clean my house while I was still in the hospital after Katherine was born. *Oh no,* I worried. *She'll see what a crummy housekeeper I am!*

But after I got over my fears of what Barb might think while scrubbing scum from my tub, I saw what a gift she was giving me. And when my parents and in-laws arrived to help out before I even left a hospital bed, I was glad they were going to see a clean house, thanks to Barb's sensitivity and kindness.

Without these relationships, my journey would perhaps have

become too stressful and lonely to bear. If we make an effort to reach out and also receive when the opportunity is before us, we can teach each other the way of wild-rose relationships. As rose branches are frequently intertwined and strengthened, so are we wrapped up in each other—giving when we can give, receiving when we need to. Friends of the heart build each other up and support each other in both dry times and downpours.

Exploring Your Story

❀ In Romans 12:15, we are told to "rejoice with those who rejoice; mourn with those who mourn." Isn't that a very practical direction when it comes to responding to the losses of our friends, reflecting the way that we hope they will respond to us? How can you apply this to your own relationships today?

❀ It's time for a field trip. If you have wild roses in your vicinity, and if it's the right time of year, take a walk until you find one to examine. Otherwise, the nearest flower shop or grocery store should offer a domestic rose to study. Take time to really look at a rose:

> *Smell its scent.*
>
> *Touch its velvety petals.*
>
> *Notice its thorns.*

❀ In your journal, draw comparisons between a beautiful rose and the relationships in your life. What provides the sweet scent? Where are the thorns of loss? How are relationships interwoven in your life? How do they contribute to fortifying your inner strength?

Inner strength is a paradox...the more we struggle to feel strong
and powerful in the loss, the more counterproductive it is.
We need to fully feel it—that we are
inadequate and incapable of going on.
Then we find a piece of ourselves and
God working though us to sustain us.
—PAM CAMPBELL

The tough resilience of wild roses has inspired my mother too. At a time of life when some retired folks are content with golf and early-bird dinners, Mom has drawn on her family history and ranching roots to write moving poems and perform them at cowboy poetry gatherings throughout the West. The beauty she discovers and creates from hard times makes her a true example of wildflower living at any stage of life. In your journal write a paragraph about your response to the images in this excerpt from "Grandma's Roses":

The men cut grandma's roses down. They said they
        blocked the view.
Where driveway met the county road, a mishap might ensue.
And then they sprayed the roots and ground, so plants
        could not regrow.

It was the Harison's Yellow rose, she'd planted long ago.

I guess they didn't know that rose had come by wagon
train.

Well-wrapped in dampened gunny sacks, it crossed the
western plain...

Those roses were our heritage as much as was the land.

It didn't matter to the men. They didn't understand...

Dad said you couldn't kill the things. I thought that he
was wrong.

I knew that little rose was tough, but prob'ly not that
strong.

Those plants withstood the wind and cold, the hail and
searing heat.

But in the face of this attack, they went down to defeat.

The sight of roses dying there had torn me up inside.

I felt as wasted as the leaves on canes they'd tossed aside.

Come spring I saw a little shoot the far side of the fence.

The Harison's rose was coming back and here was evidence.

I've come to think my family was something like that rose,

A tough and prickly people who had weathered many
blows...

And when they seemed most down and out, and all their
hope 'bout gone.

They drew strength from the land they loved and man-
aged to hang on.[3]

Eight

Sand-Lily

Hope

The delicate sand lily serves as a harbinger of spring, a promise that the earth will give forth life again. Springing from soil that looks like barren sand, it is the first sign of green I see in March as I walk along my path. Its beauty stops me in my tracks, so I pause to study the sand lily's white, translucent blossoms cupped in a handful of leaves. They remind me that God tenderly holds all our lives in his hands, gifting us with hope for the future.

Hope is such an elusive element of wildflower living. Maybe that's because for so long I tied hope to feeling instead of being. In younger days I believed hope was equal to a rush of expectation or a sense of anticipation—the trust that everything will work out in the end.

Now I know that's totally wrong. Because hope is a choice and an action based on faith, not a flimsy feeling. A life lived with hope is one based on the big picture, not on the short-term outcome of difficult circumstances. It's a daily choice to take risks and keep reaching for your dreams, even if those dreams never materialize in this life. It's a flower growing in nothing but sand, sustained by the merest moisture but sending forth its beauty nonetheless.

⁓

In my late twenties, after seven years of marriage, the time seemed right to start a family. We seemed to be late starters compared to many of our friends, but married life had been filled with change—trying to find careers, moving from Oregon to Illinois, establishing ourselves as a couple there. At last we started trying for a child. A year passed, then two. I began to read books about infertility and to visit doctors. With tests and temperatures and charts and month after month of failure, the signs of continued barrenness just added up to more mysteries.

Medical procedures grew more and more invasive: My ink-injected tubes got x-rayed; laparoscopy and hysteroscopy were performed under general anesthesia. I'd never had surgery before that or been in a hospital for anything other than visiting friends. Though I tried to fill my time with work and friends and hobbies, gradually this deep desire for a baby infused my world and dominated my days.

Infertility can be a lonely road. When you're working, you don't want the world to know you're a departure risk, so you keep quiet about trying to have a child. I never wanted to share the pain prompted by each month's period with prayer groups at church, because it seemed so personal and still somehow so vague. How would the other couples—so easily blessed with children—ever understand? I wanted something I couldn't seem to get and didn't know if I would ever have a child. I didn't even know how to ask for prayer. Each month my hope rose and then was dashed in a recurring cycle of grief.

Then I met Betsy. She and her husband, Will, also wanted a family. But with only one good fallopian tube, Betsy's options were fewer than mine. We formed a support group of two and met for lunch regularly to share ups and downs on the infertility roller coaster. She was well into fertility treatments, uncomfortable and inconvenient, when suddenly she got pregnant—with a tubal pregnancy that ended quickly and destroyed her remaining hopes of physically bearing children.

Betsy wouldn't give up her hope of becoming a mother. But she would have to take unusual steps to pursue this dream, which so many women seem to attain without effort, sometimes even without care. She knew some of these women through her career as a social worker at an adoption home for unwed mothers. Her work opened the door to entirely new ways to build a family.

> *"Though the mountains be shaken and the hills be removed,*
> *yet my unfailing love for you will not be*
> *shaken nor my covenant of peace be removed,"*
> *says the LORD, who has compassion on you.*
> *—ISAIAH 54:10*

Betsy and Will eventually became part of an unusually open adoption, which enabled them to be present for the birth of their first daughter. In fact, Will even cut the baby's cord! Three days later, at a restaurant with the birth mother after she signed the final adoption papers, the threesome—father, mother, and birth mother—were so obviously joyful, their waitress was prompted to ask what the celebration was all about. Proud Will put his arms around the women on either side of him and delightedly introduced them as "my wife," and "the mother of my child." The waitress was understandably confused.

Two years later Betsy and Will gladly adopted their daughter's biological half-sister, thus building an unconventional but much-hoped-for family.

Carl and Jenny were told as young marrieds that Jenny would never be able to physically bear a child. But in time a mission trip to India led to their adoption of a precious, doe-eyed daughter, a discarded baby literally thrown on a trash heap and rescued by one of Mother Teresa's Missionaries of Charity. Building their family (which Carl eventually tagged "The Neapolitan Gang"), they eventually adopted a blond-haired, blue-eyed son, and finally added the youngest, a chubby-cheeked charmer of African American descent. Busy raising this crew, God surprised them mightily when, at age forty, Jenny became pregnant after all and gave birth to a healthy little girl.

Through church I came to know a wonderful couple—the Martins, parents of two girls, who lost their third daughter at age two. They knew from her birth that their child would not live a long life, so in spite of their daughter's serious health problems, the Martins tried for another child. Their son was born with a rare chromosomal disorder and died soon after birth, just two months before their daughter went to heaven. Trusting in God's goodness and erring on the side of hope, they risked trying again and were blessed with a healthy son. Len and Barb Martin have five children. Two of them live in heaven.

Energetic Helen was my boss during my first years of dealing with infertility. She exemplified what a woman of faith can do because she never gave up hope that her dream of becoming a mom would become a reality, even after her fiancé chose the mission field over marriage. (Helen's serious heart condition required her to stay in the United States.) Becoming a successful career woman and business owner, Helen wanted to give a home to a child who needed one. She eventually adopted two children, both African American, an interesting challenge for a pale-skinned, middle-aged single lady living in a white-bread suburb of Chicago. Yet Helen threw herself into everything with amazing faith, asking God to let her live long enough to raise her children to adulthood. That prayer was answered. Helen became a grandmother several times over, blessed with the unique family God had made for her.

❧

I can think of so many more stories of couples who have come through infertility and the loss of a child to be blessed with the laughter of children. These men and women allowed God to use them to love and parent children despite life's barriers and losses. They clung to hope and took action based on that hope, declaring themselves on the side of life, no matter what unexpected shape it may take.

In the preceding stories, people found their prayers for children answered with children. But what about women who find similar prayers answered in a much different way? How does one express hope and gain inner strength when denied such a deep desire of the heart? My friend Pam is a woman whose life shows me the answer.

❧

I always perceived Pam as a strong person, someone who said what she thought and knew how to come through for others. She was a co-worker of mine for several years and has been an insightful, caring friend who made herself completely available during my hardest times. While she worked full time, she also wrote books and worked, along with her husband, Stan, with a church group of teenagers.

Pam told me she doesn't feel she always had true inner strength, but that "the occurrence of cancer was an initiating factor that helped me recognize the strength I do have." Her struggle with cancer in 1990 triggered those changes. "I was a strong-willed person, with a strong persona on the outside, but I felt inadequate. Cancer made me realize just how helpless I could feel, how incapacitated."

Wanting children, wanting to give and care out of a mother's heart, Pam felt her biological clock ticking. But before she could conceive, she was faced with the need for a life-saving hysterectomy. It sent her into a tailspin.

I spent the weeks following my surgery thinking and sorting through my life, not knowing what was important. I went through a long grieving process. I'd never had that kind of loss before, and it triggered a depression. I spent almost a year feeling depleted, worthless, hopeless—not caring about work.

While family and friends were supportive, I was wearing a mask to get by, feeling guilty. I had so much guilt that the cancer was my fault, that I was getting what I deserved. Of course, nobody gets cancer intentionally. But we think that we have the power to control our lives. Then when we lose that perceived power, we think, "I must be responsible," and that's where the guilt comes in.

A life-threatening illness jolts you into determining how to best spend your time. I'd always been achievement-oriented, but I now knew that wasn't important. I wanted to work with people.

At the time I knew that working with kids was the most gratifying thing in my life. It was like the honeymoon scene in *Shadowlands* where C. S. Lewis and Joy recognize that you have to take the good with the bad, as they faced the possibility of loss. I realized I couldn't fully appreciate the joy of working with kids without the loss of the possibility of having my own.

Because she survived cancer but lost the opportunity to bear children, Pam took courageous steps to change the course of her career and future. She added a master's degree program to a schedule already crammed with full-time work, freelance writing, and youth work. Her goal was to leave the publishing world and become a practicing therapist to help hurting people. After two years of hard work and a lot of sleep deprivation, Pam finally reached her goal. Today she is a clinical therapist who works with sexually traumatized adults and children. She channels her need to nurture into the daily task of fighting for them and their mental health, and she looks forward to a future of touching countless lives. In many ways she is a true parent to those who need her to fulfill that caring role.

While Pam has realized her hope for a meaningful life after cancer, she admits that it hasn't been easy, either emotionally or otherwise. "I did experience the blaming and the anger [toward God]. We fool ourselves if we don't. I was angry about losing that sense of safety and went through a period of feeling threatened. But I've found that through trauma we can get close to him."

Time has taught Pam that our hope lies in connecting with the One who can create a fragile-looking but strong sand lily that springs to life even after the harshest winter.

I used to be driven to achieve perfection....
Then loss came along and I had to figure out
what perfection meant. What is my goal now?
Wholeness is the goal,
embracing the whole self, the real self.
Strength comes out of knowing I'm working
toward wholeness and pulling all the pieces together.
—PAM CAMPBELL

God will not crush our hopes, no matter how fragile they may seem. He wants to give us the desires of our hearts. He will strengthen us to bloom in what seems like the most desolate land, the least-nurturing sand.

NURTURING SAND-LILY HOPE

What is the secret to living a hopeful life? It lies not in the circumstances you've been handed, but rather in the way you respond to those circumstances. We fall down; we get up. The sandy dust of dry times may threaten to suffocate us, and yet, like the sand lily, we find the strength to burst upward into the promise of spring.

Hope is not a happy feeling or even a mysterious gift granted to some people and not to others. Hope is a choice each of us can make in the way we build our lives after loss. We can choose to give up and give in to despair, sinking under the weight of sadness, pulled down by dreams deferred. Or we can decide to make a new life out of the pieces left to us.

The true story of Olive Ann Burns illustrates the way hope might drive us to achieve our dreams. In 1974 Olive Ann's doctor performed a blood test that indicated she was very likely to develop leukemia or lymphoma within a short time. While it was shocking news, this diagnosis wasn't completely surprising. She had lost her mother to cancer and had seen her own sister grow desperately ill from cancer treatment. Now she expected to face her own life-and-death battle.

How could a person bear such a terrible future of uncertainty, waiting to get cancer? Olive Ann formed an unexpected plan. Leaving the doctor's office, she called her husband and told him, "I may get cancer, but I am definitely going to write a novel." Olive Ann continued on with her life, struggling to tame her fears—not of death, but of chemotherapy and its possible side effects. She confronted those fears head-on when at last the dreaded cancer diagnosis materialized:

On the gray January day before she was to begin treatment,
Olive Ann knelt down and began to pray as she had never
prayed before. She knew now she could not ask God to
make her well. Instead she prayed with all her heart for
courage.... A half hour went by, and Olive Ann rose from

her knees with the realization that her prayer had been answered. The fear was gone....

Soon after the day she prayed, Olive Ann had a sudden insight into how to cope with her loss of health. On a sheet of yellow lined paper, she told herself that instead of thinking of her cancer as a *burden*, which seemed intolerable, she would think of it as a *challenge*.... Rather than resent her cancer, she would figure out a way to get through it with grace.... "When seen as the biggest challenge I had ever faced, not only the illness itself, but my attitude about it—I felt that my spiritual resources were marshaled, not beaten down."[1]

Olive Ann Burns was a housewife, a mother of two children, who decided to write a book as a way of coping with cancer. Her novel, *Cold Sassy Tree,* was published in 1984 and soon became a literary phenomenon, "taking its place alongside such American classics as *The Adventures of Tom Sawyer* and *To Kill a Mockingbird*."[2] Olive Ann became a best-selling novelist at the age of sixty, much to her own surprise. She lived another six years, continuing to write and view her illness as a challenge to be met rather than a burden to be endured. She chose hope, not hopelessness, and left a lasting mark on the world she left behind.

My Grandma Ambrose was an ordinary woman like Olive Ann Burns; though she never wrote a novel, she was a devoted wife and mother, a person with a place in her small-town community and a gift for friendship. Known for her lively spirit, Eva Ambrose was often asked to perform recitations for women's groups and other local functions. During her own battle with cancer in her last years, she chose not to withdraw from life. Instead, she worked in her garden, played bridge with her friends, rode her bike when she was able, and found peace by letting go of life's residual bitterness and disappointment. She commented that those seven years were among the best in her life as she treasured simple gifts granted by living fully each day.

> *Take all the garbage*
> *of my life*
> *Lord of the compost heap*
> *turn it into*
> *soil good soil*
> *and then plant seeds*
> *to bring forth*
> *fruit and beauty*
> *in profusion.*[3]
> —JOSEPH BAYLY, "Psalm of a Gardener"

I don't doubt that Grandma would have echoed these observations from Olive Ann Burns:

I'm convinced true fulfillment is living in God's world one day at a time, savoring it, leaving today's disappointments behind and borrowing no troubles from tomorrow. It's done

not only by accepting life, fever, and things that go bump in
the night, but also by cultivating love and new and old
friendships, and especially by finding a new work or project
that makes it exciting just to get up in the morning.[4]

Exploring Your Story

❀ Make a tribute—create an object to serve as a reminder of
what you have lost. Combine it with a symbol of hope. For
example, choose a photo of a loved one or a joyful time,
and frame it with a dried wildflower you have found. Describe your tribute in your journal, and write about what it
means to you. Or identify a "sign" that will prompt you to
choose hope over hopelessness. It might be a beautiful rock
discovered on a nature walk or a bird's feather. (After all,
Emily Dickinson described hope as "a thing with feathers.")
Keep this artifact visible, pick it up and hold it when you
feel you need to. Draw a picture of it in your journal.

❀ Remember the perfume I mentioned in chapter 6? You
may want to choose a beautiful perfume and designate it
the scent of "hope." Dab it on when you need a reminder
of your commitment to the future and your trust that God
will be there with you.

❀ The fragile sand lily points to the coming of spring. What
are the events in your life that might precede your "springtime," a time of rebirth and new beginnings? Write about
them.

❀ Record the events of a normal day, making note of the smallest incidences of hope found in your ordinary life. Write about examples of the reasons you get up in the morning and choose to get on with life.

The world is round and the place which may seem like the end may also be only the beginning.
—IVY BAKER PRIEST

Nine

Growing into the Wind

Today I write while perched on the edge of a little cliff in a garden of giant rocks. This most magnificent city park, otherwise known as the Garden of the Gods, is a vast expanse bursting with nature's glories cast in sandstone by an abundantly giving Creator. A walk in this garden, a quiet time in the midst of a busy life, is all it takes to fill me with enough soul food to last for months.

I climb to a high spot where I can look down on the untended fields below. They are filled with a profusion of flowers, grasses, and trees, growing helter-skelter where the Master Gardener has placed them. Their beauty is not that of a picture-perfect garden, the kind some people want to cultivate in their lives. Instead, their beauty is quite different—in many ways more breathtaking, more dazzling. The beautiful mess of tangled prairie-flower living might be even more lovely because no man did the work of growing it. Only God could have created such a glorious scene.

Shading the bright sun, a sturdy juniper guards me like a careful mother leaning over her sleeping baby. I wonder how any stable object can convey such tortured contortions as this tree that bends above me. It appears some mighty hand has yanked its weathered wood from pure stone and twisted it before sculpting it into this parody of an ordinary tree.

Yet I know this precarious life on a rock ledge reflects the gradual shaping of years spent steadily growing into the wind. The act of daily reaching for the sun has twirled this graying trunk into a work of art. While these gnarled branches lack the stately grace of towering ponderosa pines that dot the landscape, they speak a unique testimony to endurance in a hard place. This tree above me has much more in common with the prairie flowers in the meadow below than it does with other trees in the park.

As I study the grace of curves carved by hardship, I feel my kinship with the juniper, not the ponderosa pine. The winds of life have tried to leave me bent and weakened. Instead, they have formed a unique core of strength in my soul. I'm grateful to have experienced firsthand how God's love springs forth out of life's difficulties and provides beauty in barrenness.

When I was a young woman, my heart was usually lifted with happiness. I loved my husband, my family, my friends, my work. I felt loved in return. Sure, I discovered that most modern-day families are dysfunctional, and many people have had miserable childhoods, but I was a fortunate and rare exception in that I truly had a secure, happy, mostly unruffled childhood. There were a few tough times—like when I put a do-not-disturb sign on my swing set and

got boycotted by the neighborhood kids for my trouble—but loneliness never lasted long, and I moved from events to adventures to
new relationships with confidence that the future was a bright place.

There was a slight shadow over those early years. It did seem to
me that maybe one day I would pay a price for all this easy joy, and
I wondered if the second half of my life might indeed come crash-
ing down around me. But I didn't worry about it or give it much
thought—until the frustrating years of infertility and deferred
dreams of motherhood crept into my world. Why did I want to
have children so much when I felt content with the rest of my life?
Partly because I knew mine was a superficial life, where I slid along
on the surface of a sphere, unable to penetrate the real depths
beneath that smooth surface. I didn't want to have a controlled, easy
life; instead, I desired to live deeply and beyond my means. What
could make me lean on God more than to throw myself upon his
will and give my heart and soul to nurturing a child in a dangerous
and fallen world?

So I pursued parenthood and was granted my desire—along
with the pain and loss that attached themselves like burrs to the
pleasures of pregnancy and motherhood. It seems to be a law of
proportions: If you want the highest highs, you must reach the low-
est lows. Only then can you shatter the smooth surface of your
world and experience the blazing heat, the freezing void, the molten
rock, and all the layers of feeling that comprise real life. But is it
worth it? I would not change my life and live loss-free if it meant
never touching Katherine's soft cheek or studying the shy smiles of

my now-teenage twin sons. Pain is a high price to pay, but a fair price for all this richness.

Do you find yourself on the edge of a drop-off, wondering whether the edge will hold you or crumble beneath your feet? Do you want to cringe and crawl away—to hide from life with all its confusing complexity and uncertainty? Instead, let me encourage you to lean like the juniper into life's wind and never stop seeking the all-consuming Sun, the only Light that cuts through our deepest darkness, that prevails through any storm and drought. Your soul will be sculpted by God's hand into a dynamic work of nature's art.

Exploring Your Story

🌼 Are you open to discovering the joy of blooming in a dry place as you walk along the path of wildflower living? Look back through your journal and review the experiences in your own life that have helped you gain resilience, joy, optimism, faith, comfort, dreams, companions, hope.

🌼 *Looking back:* Choose a milestone from your past. Think about the years, months, or days since that time, then write about your answers to these questions:

  🌸 What has been the greatest lesson you have learned since that milestone experience?

  🌸 What one word best sums up your life since that experience?

  🌸 What is the most loving service you have performed since that time?

❦ What is your biggest piece of unfinished business related to that time?

❀ *Looking ahead:* Choose a day in the future that will provide a marker for you—a birthday, the start of a new year, a joyful or poignant anniversary. Consider these questions in light of the time that lies between now and that day:

❦ What advice would you give yourself about living your life between now and that future day?

❦ What do you think your biggest risk will be between today and that day?

❦ What brings you the most joy? How are you going to do or have more of that in the future?

❦ Who or what are you committed to loving and serving?

❦ What are you looking forward to learning between now and the day you have chosen?

Notes

Chapter 2: Sunflower Joy

1. Jean-Pierre de Caussade, *The Sacrament of the Present Moment* (San Francisco: HarperSanFrancisco, 1989), 47.

Chapter 3: Spiderwort Optimism

1. Dr. Lawrence LeShan, *Cancer as a Turning Point* (New York: Penguin, 1994), 7.
2. LeShan, *Cancer as a Turning Point*, 7.
3. Dr. Jon Kabat-Zinn, *Full-Catastrophe of Living: Using the Wisdom of Your Body and Mind to Face Stress, Pain, and Illness* (New York: Dell, 1990), 5.

Chapter 4: Blue-Flax Faith

1. George Matheson and Albert L. Peace, "O Love That Will Not Let Me Go," 1882 (lyrics), 1884 (music). Public Domain.

Chapter 5: Creeping-Thyme Comfort

1. Philip Yancey, *Disappointment with God* (Grand Rapids: Zondervan, 1988), 182-83.
2. Yancey, *Disappointment with God*, 200-201.

Chapter 6: Tansy-Aster Dreams

1. Anne Ellis, *Plain Anne Ellis* (Lincoln, NE, and London: University of Nebraska Press, 1997), 159-60, 163-65.

2. Ellis, *Plain Anne Ellis,* 183.

3. Stella Adler, *The Art of Acting* (New York: Applause Books, 2000), 24.

Chapter 7: Wild-Rose Companions

1. Jane M. Vogel, "No Chance to Say Good-bye," *Christian Counseling Today* 7, no. 3 (1997): 33.

2. C. S. Lewis, *A Grief Observed* (New York: Bantam, 1963), 1.

3. Jane Ambrose Morton, "Grandma's Roses," *Turning to Face the Wind* (Phoenix: Cowboy Miner Productions, 2003), 187-89. Reprinted by permission. All rights reserved.

Chapter 8: Sand-Lily Hope

1. A reminiscence contained in Olive Ann Burns and Katrina Kenison, *Leaving Cold Sassy: The Unfinished Sequel to Cold Sassy Tree* (New York: Ticknor and Fields, 1992), 185-89.

2. Burns and Kenison, *Leaving Cold Sassy,* vii.

3. Joseph Bayly, "Psalm of a Gardener," *Psalms of My Life* (Elgin, IL: David C. Cook, 1987), 15. Reprinted by permission. All rights reserved. Reproduction prohibited.

4. Burns and Kenison, *Leaving Cold Sassy,* 192.